# Praise For

# The Bible vs Theology

I find John's analysis of local beliefs in *The Bible vs Theology* intriguing, as they shape strong religious identities worldwide. This book highlights the indispensable roles theology and biblical study play in expanding our comprehension of God, surpassing futile attempts to know Him. It examines the intricate relationship between theology and the bible's content, presenting innovative insights on how this connection deepens our understanding of God, in contrast to scientific, philosophical, agnostic, humanistic, and religious viewpoints.

What's most captivating is how the book explores the similarities and differences in the Bible's content and theological exploits, empowering us to further explore God. A must-read book for anyone seeking to understand and navigate theological ideologies without compromising their faith in Christ.

*Pastor Patrick Igbinigie*
*Founder Victorious Faith Mission*
*Hands For Africa Advancement Network,*
*Mauritania, West Africa*

\*\*\*

I now realize that the lack of research materials comparing the Bible's content and theological explorations is concerning, especially in light of the growing threat of false doctrines. This book, *The Bible vs Theology*, provides a clear and concise examination of the Bible and the theologies it inspires, effectively showing how they complement each other, emphasizing the benefits of understanding their roles.

This research has benefits that extend beyond the intended audience, making it a valuable and timely contribution to the body of Christ. I specifically recommend this book to all Bible students, urging them to read it with an open mind and the Holy Spirit's assistance for maximum insights.

***Rev. Appolonia C. Okwu***
***Chief Executive Director***
***Random Grace Mission***
***Nigeria***

\*\*\*

An important book I want believers to read to learn more about biblical and theological facts. A must read especially for believers in active/street evangelism.

This remarkable book delves into the authenticity of the word of God and is highly recommended and is a book I find difficult to take a break while reading. I couldn't stop turning pages to see what special thoughts were next. It's interesting to know that a believer studying the Bible daily might not even know what the first five books of the Old Testament are called. Don't miss out!

*Pastor Osas*
*RCCG Solution Center Church*
*Stockholm, Sweden*

*** 

This is a very informative and educative book for all that aspire to know more about God. It is very interesting to read, difficult to stop once you start and leaves you hungry for more of God's Word. The author's ability to distinguish between the Bible and theology creates a balance which makes the book a must read for pastors, teachers of the Word, and all believers.

We look forward to having volume 2 soon.

*Pastor Jerry John Momodu*
*Zonal Pastor*
*Redeemed Christian Church of God*
*Life Centre Västerås, Sweden.*

*** 

This book in your hands gives invaluable inroads into the bare-bones of truth and life itself with an eye-opening easy-to-grasp insight to the intricacies of the highly misconstrued and often misrepresented notion in many Christian circles of *The Bible vs Theology*, in a manner that both the layman and the informed mind can perceive.

The writer effortlessly highlights the differences and similarities in a simple and clear way that everyone can understand, regardless of their level of expertise or spiritual journey. The book avoids getting tangled in intricate jargon and terminology frequently connected with the study of these topics.

John's presentation style of the subject matter is not just disarming but inviting at the same time and seems to take away the inherent fear often associated with the perceived complexity in the subjects. He caringly and boldly handholds one through the forest on this explorative journey of enlightenment. This makes for a reassuringly pleasurable read.

It is my sincere belief and earnest hope that every open-minded, honest seeker of truth who comes in contact with this material will be genuinely transformed, having the scales of confusion veiling their minds completely fall off from their spiritual eyes of understanding brought about by the gradual clarity in the pages of this book.

This piece is a must read for all and sundry.

*Pastor Tillarh Mukasa*
*Resident Pastor*
*RCCG Solution Centre*

*Stockholm Sweden*
*Asst. Pastor-in-charge of Province 1*
*RCCG Europe Region 3*
*Sundbyberg, Sweden*

\*\*\*

This book, *The Bible vs Theology,* you are holding in your hand right now is a blessing and a life-changing material that will help you in the journey of your life. The book is well arranged and easy to read; the content is fantastic, intriguing, enlightening and eye-opening. The author has done a due diligence to distinguish between the Bible and theology: What they mean, their similarities and differences. He delved also into types and branches of theology as instruments to help understand the Bible. This piece of material you are about to read is Holy Spirit inspired and it brings clarity to how theology should add value to the Bible and is not a replacement for the Bible.

One of my takeaways from this book is that the Bible is sufficient on its own and it is authored by God through men while theology on the other hand is dependent on the Bible for it to have meaning and cause positive impact in people's life. A Holy Spirit inspired theology illuminates the heart of men when it is applied. Unfortunately, there are theologian today who do not have the special revelation of God - they are not born again hence they end up bringing more confusions into the body of Christ. The author – Bro.

John Woloko is a born again and Spirit filled theologian, his work speaks for him by the way.

I strongly recommend this book for you and everyone out there who desires to know more about God and the Bible. This book will enhance your life and boost your knowledge on the subject matter and your walk with the Lord will never remain the same.

*Pastor Taiwo Ajayi*
*Special Assistant to Continental Overseer*
*[Discipleship and Quality Training]*
*The Redeemed Christian Church of God, Europe*

# THE BIBLE VS THEOLOGY

## LIGHTING THE WAY

*John Mwafise Woloko*

Published by KHARIS PUBLISHING, an imprint of
KHARIS MEDIA LLC.

Copyright © 2024 John Mwafise Woloko

ISBN-13: 978-1-63746-250-8

ISBN-10: 1-63746-250-6

Library of Congress Control Number: 2024933021

All KHARIS PUBLISHING products are available at
special quantity discounts for bulk purchase for sales
promotions, premiums, fund-raising, and educational
needs. For details, contact:

Kharis Media LLC
Tel: 1-630-909-3405
support@kharispublishing.com
www.kharispublishing.com

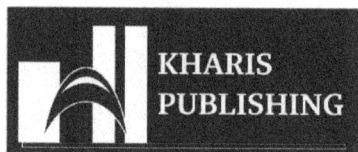
KHARIS PUBLISHING

# DEDICATION

Written for

New converts and immature Christians.

Bible and theology students.

Christians who struggle with denominationalism and divisions in the Body of Christ.

Non-believers hesitant to embrace the Christian faith because they are confused about Christian movements they encounter.

# ACKNOWLEDGMENTS

To my lovely wife, Amaya: You spent more time with the children the Christmas week I wrote this book. I dedicate it to you.

# CONTENTS

# INTRODUCTION

Unbelievers often asked me this question during street evangelism in Basel: "Why is there disagreement among Christians?"

I used to play the intellectual game and confidently state that every group in the world has disagreements. It became clear that my answer didn't convince any of them. While reflecting on the inability of these unbelievers to comprehend it, I discovered a flaw in my response: I claimed to speak for a God who is pure, all-powerful, and holy. Why would this God allow confusion among His people? The pursuit of suitable answers led me to an area we didn't sufficiently explore; the Bible and the theologies it generates.

Is there any difference between the Bible and theology? Ask this question to Christians at random, and these are some of the answers you'll get:

"Theology is the study of the Bible."

"Theology explains the Bible better."

"I guess they are the same."

"I don't know."

"There shouldn't be a big difference between them."

"The Bible and theology contain God's revelations."

"I never thought about this question."

"They help each other?"

"Our pastor said theology helps to understand the mysteries in God's Word."

The truth is, many Christians haven't considered this question, yet it's important to understand the relationship between the Bible and theology in your Christian walk. And you have to take it seriously. Believe it or not, most of the unhelpful polemics in the Christian faith stem from misunderstanding this relationship.

Should we call this study philosophical? What's philosophy in the first place? From a non-technical viewpoint, we can say philosophy brings meaning to life. Dr. Johnson says, "It shows what is what, and therefore, everyone should know enough of it to carry on successfully and productively in life. This is more so for the Christian believer."[1]

We want to know what is what between the Bible and theology in this book. So, yes, this study is philosophical, given that we want to make meaning out of two supposedly distinct things. Let's take them into

---

[1] *Dr. Johnson, Philosophy, 3.*

the philosophical lab, perform a thorough dissection of the components of each and make deductions that enable us to make better use of them in our Christian walk.

Because philosophical thoughts have no limits, we need to define the boundaries of this study so we don't dive into an unprofitable exercise. The study is theistic. What do I mean by that? As Christians, we believe in God, who guides our reasoning process. He enables us to make genuine deductions from what we observe in the material and non-material worlds around us. When we put together the knowledge we gain, we build trustworthy theologies. Far better, because God guides us, we make rightful use of the knowledge we gain and live a life of purpose.

Therefore, this book follows a simple format. The first chapter looks at what the Bible is. Chapter Two defines and introduces the branches of theology. In Chapters Three and Four, we look into the similarities between theology and the Bible and the reasons God allows theological explorations. Then, Chapter Five explores the differences between them. The sixth chapter looks into how we can make the best use of both. Then, we finish with a practical approach to interpreting the Bible in Chapter Seven.

We hope to achieve the following by the end of this study:

- Give the Bible its rightful authority.
- Learn to distinguish between the Logos and rhema.
- Understand how to identify good theology.
- Discover the correct relationship between the Bible and theology.
- Determine when to seek help from the field of theology.

Are you ready for this exercise? Flip through the pages. May the Good Lord refresh your mind with excellent knowledge, in Jesus' Name, Amen!

Chapter one

# THE BIBLE

## THE NAME BIBLE

The English word "Bible" comes from two Ancient Greek words, *biblos* and *biblion*. Both words mean "book" or "roll." In those days, people used papyrus plants that "grew in marshes or riverbanks, primarily along the Nile"[2] to make these writing materials. Latin-speaking Christians used "the plural form biblia to denote all books of the Old and New Testaments."[3]

Nowadays, we have other names we use for the Bible. We use the word Scripture to denote all the books that make up the sacred writings of the Bible. A good example is in Matthew 21:42, "Jesus said to them, "Have you not read the Scriptures?" Depending on the context, Bible figures used the singular form Scripture to denote the sacred writings: "For what does Scripture

---

[2] *Dr. Saneesh, Bible Introduction, 28–29.*
[3] *Dr. Saneesh, Bible Introduction, 2.*

say? "Abraham believed God, and it was accounted to him for righteousness" (Romans 4:3). "All Scripture is given by inspiration of God…" (2 Timothy 3:16). Other times, the same singular form, scripture, refers to a verse or specific passage. "Have you not read this scripture…" (Mark 12:10).

"The Word of God" is another title to denote the sacred writings. We use this term to stress the fact that the sacred writings in the Bible are revelations from God Himself. Again, depending on the context, the Word of God can mean the entire sacred writings, a verse, or a section of the Bible.

Other phrases we use for the sacred writings are Testament, The Law, The Oracles of God, The Law and the Prophets, God's Precepts, God's Commands, God's Judgments, God's Word, God's Decrees, Testimonies, Holy Scriptures, Sacred Scriptures, The Law of the Lord, Word of Christ, Writing of Truth, and Book of the Lord. Some of these phrases can mean a single passage in the Bible or its entirety. It depends on how we use them.

## THE BIBLE'S STRUCTURE

The Bible is a book, but what type of book? Each book has its peculiarities. Let's explore the unique characteristics of the Bible. The entire Bible comprises 66 unique books. These 66 books fall into two sections or Testaments. The word Testament comes from the Latin word *testamentum*, which means "a will, testimony, or witness."[4] The first part, the Old Testament, comprises 39 books. The other, the New Testament, has 27 books. Altogether, the entire Bible has 1189 chapters and roughly 31,173 verses. The number of verses can vary slightly depending on the language into which we translate the Bible.

The next thing we discover is those who wrote the Bible did so in a timeframe of 1500 to 1600 years. That's over 40 generations. It gets more interesting to learn that 40 authors wrote the books of the Bible during this period. Most of these authors didn't see or know each other. Moses, who wrote the first books of the Old Testament, lived a thousand years before Paul wrote his letters.

Another fascinating thing to note is the profiles of these authors. They are from all walks of life. Moses was a top political figure trained in an Egyptian institution (Acts 7:22). David and his son, Solomon, were kings and poets, Peter a fisherman, Matthew a tax collector, Amos a herdsman, Daniel a prime minister, Joshua a military general, Nehemiah a cupbearer to the king of Babylon, Luke a physician or doctor, and Paul a rabbi.

---

[4] *Encyclopaedia, Testament, 1–12.*

Just when you think it can't get better comes the place and state each author was in as he wrote. Moses wrote in the wilderness, and Luke did while traveling. John was on the Island of Patmos, Paul inside the prison walls, Jeremiah in the dungeon, and Daniel on a hillside in a palace. "David wrote in times of war, James in acute persecution, Solomon in peaceful moments, and Jude in the presence of many false teachers. Therefore, some wrote in the heights of joy, others in the depths of sorrow and despair."[5]

The diversity above means the authors wrote in different ways. We can identify five main writing styles in the Old Testament. The first five books, Genesis, Exodus, Leviticus, Numbers and Deuteronomy, are Law books. Greeks called them the Pentateuch. The Hebrews refer to them as the Torah. Then come the historical books, Joshua, Judges, Ruth, 1 and 2 Samuel, 1 and 2 Kings, 1 and 2 Chronicles, Ezra, Nehemiah and Esther.

The authors of Job, Psalms, Proverbs, Ecclesiastes and Song of Songs used a poetic language. The remaining books are prophetic. We identify two types of prophets: Major prophets include Isaiah, Jeremiah, Lamentations, Ezekiel, and Daniel. The others are the minor prophets, Hosea, Joel, Amos, Obadiah, Jonah,

---

[5] *Dr. Saneesh, Bible Introduction, 3.*

Micah, Nahum, Habakkuk, Zephaniah, Haggai, Zechariah, and Malachi.

The labels major and minor do not imply the major prophets are greater than the minor. Major prophets had a much longer career and more voluminous literature. Prophet Isaiah, for instance, wrote 66 chapters, Jeremiah wrote 52 chapters plus the Book of Lamentations. The careers of the minor prophets were shorter, with less voluminous literature. Hosea has 14 chapters, Joel 3, Amos 9, and Obadiah only 1.

The Law books help us understand things about God's pattern of morality. They also have a considerable amount of historical information. Genesis, for instance, teaches about the history of creation. Exodus gives us thorough knowledge of the history of God's people among the Egyptians.

Historical books help us trace our lives back in time. Poetic books add meaning to the practical experiences we face in life. The major and minor prophets warn people of certain habits in life and foretell things that will come to pass in the near and far future. Many things major and minor prophets foretold happened already. Some are yet to happen.

In the New Testament, we commonly refer to the books of Matthew, Mark, Luke, and John as the Gospels. These books teach us about the life, ministry, death, and resurrection of Jesus Christ. Their purpose is to lead you to believe that Jesus is the Christ, the Son of God. The book of Acts is the only purely historical book in the New Testament. It tells how the church began and fulfilled Christ's commission to spread the gospel throughout the entire world. Romans, 1 and 2 Corinthians, Galatians, Ephesians, Philippians, Colossians, 1 and 2 Thessalonians, 1 and 2 Timothy, Titus, Philemon, Hebrews, James, 1 and 2 Peter, 1, 2 and 3 John, and Jude are letters. They contain important doctrines. Their main purpose is to help us practice a Christ-like lifestyle. Revelation is the only purely prophetic book in the New Testament. It is loaded with promises to those who endure the hardships of living a life of faith who stay faithful until the return of Jesus Christ.

The Bible doesn't cease to fascinate. Did you know its authors wrote on three different continents? Yes, Africa, Asia, and Europe. This means diverse languages and cultural settings. The authors wrote in three languages: Hebrew, Greek, and Aramaic. Authors of the Old Testament wrote mostly in Hebrew. That was the most common language of their time. Greek was "the international language at the time of Christ."[6] The Babylonian captivity of the Jews caused them to embrace the Greek language. Aramaic "was the common language of the Near East until the time of Alexander the great (6th century B.C. to 4th century

[6] *Dr. Saneesh, Bible Introduction, 4.*

B.C).”[7] 2 Kings 18:26-28; Isaiah 36:11; Nehemiah 13:24; Isaiah 19:18; Revelation 9:11, 16:16; Genesis 14:13.

The Bible's message touches all classes of people: old, young, rich, poor, wise, simple, high, and low. "It is not the oldest book, but the authors wrote its first part over 3500 years ago and the last part nearly 2000 years ago.[8]" "The Bible is more popular than any modern book. It was the first book to be printed in AD 1450."[9] The printing press, which allowed mass production of books, was first used then. It was and remains a bestseller. Some parts of the Bible count "over 2062 language translations."[10] The entire Bible has been translated into "over 200 languages."[11] "Although the Bible is an oriental and foreign book, it has transcended all national boundaries and is received by all peoples as their very own book."[12]

Authors of the Bible wrote on stones, wooden tablets, clay tablets, animal skin, parchment, vellum, papyrus, and paper. They used chisels, metal styluses, and pen and ink to record the words of the Bible. Today, the

[7] *Dr. Saneesh, Bible Introduction, 4.*
[8] *Dr. Saneesh, Bible Introduction, 5*
[9] *Dr. Saneesh, Bible Introduction, 5*
[10] *Dr. Saneesh, Bible Introduction, 6*
[11] *Dr. Saneesh, Bible Introduction, 6*
[12] *Dr. Saneesh, Bible Introduction, 7*

Bible exists in audio, electronic, and digital forms as well.

We can't mention every aspect of the Bible's structure here. We could, in another book, talk about the history of its assemblage into 66 books; the difficulties encountered during its translation into other languages; how our forefathers preserved it over the years until this day; the copies of copies of the original manuscripts, and the discovery of the Dead Sea Scrolls.

Note that there is a list of other books called the Pseudepigrapha and Apocrypha, but their exact number and distinction is unclear. The term 'Pseudepigrapha' originates from the Greek words 'pseudo' (false, untrue) and 'graphia' (writing, description). 'Apocrypha' is a Greek phrase derived from 'apokryphos', meaning "hidden; obscure, or hard to understand."[13] These books are "distinctly spurious and inauthentic in their overall content."[14] They "claim to have been written by Biblical authors but express religious fancy and magic."[15] These books have "dreams, visions and revelations in the apocalyptic style of Ezekiel, Daniel and Zechariah."[16]

The argument for not including them in the Bible is that Jesus and the apostles did not quote from them,

[13] *Online, Etimomogy Dictionary*
[14] *Dr. Saneesh, Bible Introduction, 12*
[15] *Dr. Saneesh, Bible Introduction, 12*
[16] *Dr. Saneesh, Bible Introduction, 13*

but some scholars say God inspired a few of the books in the Apocrypha. We clearly see Jude quotes from the Book of Enoch, but this debate is not relevant to our study. The reader can research it from other sources or check the Douay-Rheims/Catholic Bible, which includes the chapters of the Apocrypha if interested.

## THE BIBLE'S DIVINE TOUCH

From the Bible's structure, we laid a good foundation on which we can build to learn more about other mysteries of the book. Think about everything we have learned so far. Let me remind you of a few: different authors wrote the Bible in various locations over a period of 1500 to 1600 years. These authors came from all walks of life and wrote under diverse conditions, depending on their context. The authors wrote in three different languages. We have translated the Bible into over 200 languages today, and it remains the most popular book out there. What fascinates us the most? The 66 books of the Bible point to one theme—Jesus.

Pause a minute and reflect on this. How could that be? How could people of such diversity, who, for the most part, didn't know each other and were writers of quite different epochs, all point in the same direction? And how could that happen without someone organizing the whole thing over the generations?

There's only one logical conclusion: It has nothing to do with luck, fate, serendipity, or chance. It is the hand of God. The "very existence of such a book is proof that the Bible is not of man, but that it is a production of God."[17] And the Bible has an awesome quality. It testifies about its origin from God and the authenticity of its content. Second Peter 1:21 says, "Holy men of God spoke as they were moved by the Holy Spirit." In 2 Timothy 3:16, we read, "All Scripture is given by inspiration of God…"

Therefore, the message of the Bible is without contradiction and is united in theme because God is its true inspirer and author. Over 2000 times in the Bible, God claims to be its author. He uses the phrase, "Thus says the Lord." There's no other book out there that matches such claims.

Anyone who reads the Bible with an open mind can understand its message, but the knowledge in a single chapter is endless. "The highest intellect cannot grasp all its meaning. People have written great volumes on single verses."[18] Yet, the same verses continue to inspire our generations. Besides, "history shows that mighty kings, emperors, and priests tried to destroy the Bible. They died, but the Bible lives on."[19] Over the years, the Bible suffered "the blows of men who

---

[17] *Dr. Saneesh, Bible Introduction, 13*

[18] *Dr. Saneesh, Bible Introduction, 14*

[19] *Dr. Saneesh, Bible Introduction, 13*

believed that it was not inspired by God but was full of human errors. These men pass away, but the Bible continues."[20] Other men and women endured persecution, suffered many things, and even died in testifying about its authenticity.

Despite the alarming evidence supporting its authenticity, those who put their trust in the worldly system still reject the Bible. Western societies that relied on the Bible's content enjoyed great peace and spiritual prosperity. These days, they remove it from their public schools. Many of these societies gradually embraced the destructive values of the world's system. They accept the theory of evolution as their guide. See what goes on in these countries; pagan practices including legalizing homosexuality and abortion! Yet, the Bible stands strong and tall; its wisdom and knowledge remain a blessing for those who seek divine truth and live according to it.

## THE BIBLE'S CONTENT

Most of what I have mentioned so far about the Bible is external evidence of its authenticity. Let's look at what is inside it. We start with its claims. We saw a little about this in the last section. Merly reading the Bible's content challenges your thought life. It explicitly or implicitly claims to be the Word of God. "Thus says

[20] *Dr. Saneesh, Bible Introduction, 13*

29

the Lord..." "God said..." (see Exodus 14:1; 20:1; Leviticus 4:1; Numbers 4:1; Deuteronomy 4:2; 32:48; Isaiah 1:10, 24; Jeremiah 1:11; Ezekiel 1:3).

Peter tells us God inspired everything the prophets prophesied (2 Peter 1:16-21). Paul clearly saw the things he wrote as "commandments from the Lord" (1 Corinthians 14:37). The believers Paul evangelized accepted the things he said and wrote as "the Word of God" (1 Thessalonians 2:13). John says the apostles were God's spokesmen (1 John 4:6). Prophet Jeremiah received his message directly from God (Jeremiah 1:4-5; 11:1-3). The psalmist confirms the words of the Bible are God-breathed (Psalm 19:7-11). The claims God inspired the authors of the Bible are too many. We can't go through all of them here.

The Bible introduces the concept of revelation. Revelation is the act of God unveiling Himself to humankind. There are two ways God reveals Himself to humankind. The first is through general or natural revelation. These are things about God everyone can have access to. Many of them relate to creation. The psalmist says, "The heavens declare the glory of God; and the firmament shows His handiwork" (Psalm 19:1).

Who is not amazed by nature? All you need to do is to look into a clear night sky. A few months ago, we hiked on the Grindelwald, a famous village in the Swiss Alps. On one of those gigantic glacial peaks, we observed parchments of clouds beneath, cutting across endless undulations. The colorful separation of forest and farmlands overlaid the mountains, descending to the banks of glacial lakes. There are no words to describe such natural beauty. Yes, that's God's handiwork. No human in his or her right senses can stay indifferent to these natural wonders. Yet, we deal with a world God destroyed by a great flood in the days of Noah. How was the earth in the days of Adam and Eve before the flood?

Astronomers are nowhere close to understanding the universe. We can't access most parts of the deep. But with a simple "breath of His nostrils," God can uncover the great seas and make their foundations bear (Psalm 18:15). What about the work of man's hands? Remember, God created us in His image, even those who reject the invitation into His kingdom. Every human being on earth exhibits some of God's attributes. He gave us wisdom and intelligence that far exceed what we see in other living creatures.

Human beings can tame lions, elephants, and whales despite their great physical strengths and sizes. We have invented machines that bring us from one part of the globe to another in a few hours. Others take us to parts of the solar system in days. The skyscrapers, sea boats, cars, trains, industrial machines, infrastructure, transportation network—we do all these things with the wisdom God gave us.

He gave Noah wisdom to build an ark (Genesis 6), Cain built an entire city (Genesis 4:17), Solomon built a wonderful temple (1 Kings 6), and ordinary people built the Tower of Babel (Genesis 11:1-9). All these are directly or indirectly the work of God's hands. We can't match God's ability to design and create. But every human being inherited a natural gift or talent from Him. Human inventions never cease to amaze us. God uses all these things to reveal Himself to us naturally.

Nonetheless, the Bible also talks of special revelation. Whereas everyone can access general or natural revelation, special revelation is not for everyone. "The nature of this mode of revelation is that it consists primarily of words. There are three elements to special revelation: specific times, specific modes, and specific persons."[21]

The Bible teaches us we need special revelation because of our sinful state. Paul writes, "for all have sinned and fall short of the glory of God" (Romans 3:23). The principal reason for God's special revelations is to deliver us from sin. We can't find the solution to sin outside of God's special revelation.

Natural revelation can't solve sin, either. "The human mind is so corrupt, and human wisdom is so marred by sin that no human, howsoever great, can discover or perceive spiritual truths through any human process of

[21] *Keathley, Bibliology, 12*

meditation. Thus, once again, it is erroneous and even heretical to suggest that spiritual truths identical to that of the Bible have been recorded in books produced by non-Christian sages and ascetics"[22]

Hence, the entire message of the Bible, as we saw before, points to God's salvation plan for humankind in Jesus. The Old and New Testaments join hands coherently to reveal God's victorious way out of the sin that entangles us. And Jesus gives us the command, "Go into all the world and preach the gospel to every creature. He who believes and is baptized will be saved; but he who does not believe will be condemned" (Mark 16:15-16).

Although God's special revelation comes principally through words, He can also use other methods to reveal Himself. He does this through dreams, visions, angels, and events. We find all these methods and more in the Bible.

## REASONS FOR THE BIBLE

Earlier, we saw the Bible talks about its content. It explains and interprets itself. For most of what we need to know in life concerning spiritual matters and understanding the state of the world or universe, we don't need to go far away from the Bible's content. It talks about everything in amazing detail. A lifetime is

---

[22] *Dr. Saneesh and Dr. Johnson, Word of God, 8*

not enough to grasp all of its teachings on every subject. If we concentrate enough on studying its content, we will not find ourselves in all the confusion the world creates.

The Bible talks about its purpose for being; we see that in 2 Timothy 3:16–17, "All Scripture is given by inspiration of God, and is profitable for doctrine, for reproof, for correction, for instruction in righteousness, that the man of God may be complete, thoroughly equipped for every good work." This is the value and purpose of God's special revelations. The Word of God in the Bible does just what it says. Let's get into these four reasons the Bible talks of.

The first reason God gave us the Bible is for ***doctrine***. What is doctrine? The word doctrine comes from the Greek word *didaskalia*, which means teaching or learning. Another question arises. What doctrines does the Bible teach? Again, the Bible itself answers this question. All you have to do is read through the Bible, and you discover God gives specific directives for things concerning our lives. There's a way God wants us to behave in a family, in church, at work, with unbelievers, with brothers and sisters in Christ, and so on. He has prerequisites for those who want to marry and the manner in which we approach marriage. The Father tells us how to use our finances, what to do in times of joy or troubles, and in fact, He leaves no subject out.

So, the things God says about a subject—let's say, living a holy life—make up its doctrine. That is what we have to learn and practice on the subject. Therefore, doctrine "refers to God's fundamental principles for man's life, both eternal and abundant. It gives us the basics, the fundamental truths upon which life is to be built."[23]

The second reason God gave us the Bible is for ***reproof*.** We derived the word reproof from the Greek *elegchos*, which means proof or conviction. We first need a personal, unshakable conviction that what God says in the Bible is the absolute truth. When we establish this in our hearts, we can learn to distinguish between what God wants and what He doesn't, based on our study of the Bible. Then comes the third and critical stage, which is to show proof or bring a godly argument that convicts those who don't walk by the Scriptures. Most believers engage in reproofing when they confront someone from another worldview. You will discover reproof is the core of apologetics when we deal with theology.

The third reason God gave us the Bible is for ***correction.*** Most of us understand what the act of correcting is. The word comes from the Greek *epanorthosis*, which means "a straightening up again." But God wants us to correct based on what He wrote

---

[23] *Keathley, Bibliology, 17*

in the Bible. To correct means to bring someone who is off course back on course.

In our normal lives on earth, we receive correction from our parents, guardians, or superiors. Whenever we do things that are contrary to what they say, they engage us in some corrective measures. God does the same with us. He has a reason for creating us and has a purpose for our lives. When we receive Jesus in our lives, we become God's children with a godly purpose to advance His kingdom. Every time we deviate from our life's purpose, He corrects us.

There are many ways He corrects us. As we read His Word, the Holy Spirit shows us the right things to do in every endeavor. When we don't pay attention to His Word in the Bible (by not reading the Bible or spending time to meditate on His Word), He uses spiritual leaders, ordinary believers, or even angels, dreams, and visions to correct us. If we still don't respond to these methods of correction, God can use the circumstances of life to teach us His truth and bring us back on track. The Bible says in Proverbs 3:11–12, "My son, do not despise the chastening of the Lord, nor detest His correction. For whom the Lord loves He corrects, just as a father the son in whom he delights."

The fourth and last reason God gave us the Bible is for ***instruction in righteousness***. The Greek word used here is *paideia*, which means "education or training, disciplinary correction." Humans have a natural tendency to do things that violate God's principles. Even when we become children of God, the world still has a significant influence on us. It takes time to overcome the old habits and embrace the new life in Christ.

God wants us to develop discipline in every area of life. For this reason, He gives us instructions to follow in our undertakings. Hidden in those instructions is the divine wisdom and knowledge that enables us to navigate through the issues of life. The difference between God's instructions and all others is that His are righteous ones. God's righteous instructions motivate us to do His perfect will for us and they enable us to live a fulfilled life on earth. The psalmist says it better, "Your word I have hidden in my heart, that I might not sin against You" (Psalm 119:11).

## BIBLE DEFINITION

So, what exactly is the Bible? The first thing we note is the Bible is a book—but not just any type. It is a book God Himself wrote. That's the difference between the Bible and all other books out there. God doesn't claim He wrote any other book except the Bible. Sure, He wrote the Bible indirectly through men, but that removes nothing from its authenticity. Sometimes, He spoke, and his authors wrote. Other times, He inspired them with the Holy Spirit's help to record what would be useful for us.

The second thing we see is God uses the Bible to reveal Himself to us. The Bible has God's message to humankind. He recorded all His plans to deliver us from all the traps of sin. We discover our purposes for being in this world from the Bible. If we believe and accept this message, God sees us as His children and uses us to do specific things that bring glory to His Name. No other book or religion offers this type of relationship with its audience and adherents.

As a third point, God's message in the Bible never gets old. It has the power to transform and touch every generation. People write books for specific audiences, but no one can stay indifferent after reading the Bible with an open heart. It either convinces or provokes you. It touches the rich, poor, young, old, famous, weak, strong, leader, servant, high or low-status; it exempts none. In the Bible, God reveals Himself as God the Father, Son and Holy Spirit, yet He is One. His Name is Jesus, a mystery that troubles many a philosopher. But God brings satisfaction and peace to the simple and humble in heart.

Fourth, the Bible is the most important book you can find on earth. Of course, many authors claim their book is the best and contains the truth. Muslims claim the Quran came directly from God, unaltered by humans. Buddhists have enormous volumes of spiritual materials they claim bring humans to fulfillment. Atheists have countless books on the market. None of these can match the Bible. Why?

First, just like Jesus, the Bible humbles itself in the way it unveils God to us. Jesus' disciples had in their hearts something the Jews in Israel believe until this day: That the Messiah would come, conquer the Romans, establish Himself as king, and rule with them. But Jesus, although the King of kings, didn't come as a king. He was born in a lowly manger; not even one inn in an entire city had room for Him. But that little Man in the manger is God Himself, the Creator of life and everything. In the same manner, God used imperfect men to write and compile the Bible. The common man or woman overlooks its message, but let that message confront you—it's fire.

Second, none of those other books out there solve the sin problem, the fundamental problem of all humans. The Bible is the only book that brings a solution to sin in Jesus, and it stands out primarily because of that.

### REMARKS

There's much more we can say about the Bible, but we've gone through enough to lay the foundation for what the Bible is. Now, you know the Bible comes from God. You saw the type of people He used to write it and the information He reveals. We also looked into the reasons God gives us the Bible, the uniqueness of its content, and why no book in the world compares to it.

Please pay attention to all you have learned so far about the Bible. Hold that at the back of your mind as you continue reading. In the next chapter, we discuss what theology is. As you study theology, reflect on how it is similar to the Bible or differs from it. We'll expose the principal similarities and differences in the third chapter.

Chapter Two

# THEOLOGY

## WHAT IS THEOLOGY

The name theology comes from two Greek words, *theos* and *Logos*. Theos means "God," Logos means "word," "reason," or "plan." If we put them together, theology is the study of God's Word, but because God reveals Himself in the Bible as the Word, theology is the study of God and His relationship to humankind. We discovered in Chapter One that God makes Himself known to humankind through natural and special revelations. Theology simply looks into the details of these revelations.

Theology is a universal exercise. Stanford E. Murrell, ThD says, "…every thoughtful individual is a theologian to some extent, for life and destiny are affected by what an individual believes about God and His will."[24] You just can't run away from the whole idea

---

[24] *Murrell, Systematic Theology, 20*

of God's existence. Some try to occupy themselves with drugs, work, riches, the pleasures of this world, and even intellectual knowledge, but every human being seeks to understand the meaning of life. The absence of a satisfactory answer creates a gap within. Humans engage in all sorts of activities; we toil day and night in a quest to fill this gap.

Solomon says, "I have seen the works that are done under the sun; and indeed, all is vanity and grasping for the wind" (Ecclesiastes 1:14). Eventually, busy humans catch themselves in their own contemplations, reasoning in all directions. This inspired A. W. Tozer to say, "Nothing twists and deforms the soul more than a low or unworthy conception of God."[25] Yes, the whole essence of this reasoning is to fill a gap in oneself only God can fill. This opens the door to an unending exploration process—the quest for knowledge.

This desire and thirst for knowledge to make meaning out of life has its own realities. In fact, it has caused the human mind to become a battleground for ideas. All human minds confront fierce competition for ideas, each wanting to settle in with the promise to fill that gap.

Humans have developed many worldviews as a result, but truth and fulfillment remain a mystery. To arrive at

[25] *Tozer, Pursuit Of God, 135*

the truth, one must play fair, as stated by Dr. Johnson C. Philip, ThD, PhD:

> When ideas are available for cross-examination, true and wholesome ideas prevail. However, the moment the privilege for critical examination is taken away from the common man, an academic or even an administrative elite is created to control, approve, and disseminate ideas. What they approve of becomes the new corpus of right thought, and what they disapprove automatically is rejected. Whether the rejected ideas are right or wrong no longer matters.[26]

Therefore, in simple language, we can say theology is the act of studying God and His message to humankind. In greater detail, it is a method by which we seek and reason about God, His Word, and His will for humankind, organizing information and gathering evidence to understand Him better.

## THEOLOGY, A BATTLE FOR IDEAS

People have used various methods to understand God and His will for humankind. Some have studied so much they arrived at the conclusion there is no God. Others don't know which camp to adhere to. Waves of ideas from every direction constantly sweep them.

[26] *Dr. Johnson, What Is Philosophy, 4*

Even among those who claim to know God, not all have a stable faith. In their book *Towards A Christian Worldview*, Gary Crampton, ThD and Richard E. Bacon, ThD, say, "The first thing many Christians lack is a coherent worldview. The question is not so much whether we have a philosophy of life but what that philosophy will be."[27]

This brings me to my tribe's people, the Bakweries, of Cameroon. They've got some traditional beliefs and core values they adhere to. Babila Mutia, a researcher, summarized those beliefs in the research journal, *Cahiers D'Etudes Africaines*:

> Among the Bakweri, the natural and supernatural worlds interact constantly in all aspects of life. In this regard, they have a three-dimensional view of the cosmos in which the supernatural world, the world of the ancestors, and the world of the living are in frequent interaction.[28]

When we were young, people in my village always performed certain rituals in honor of what they called "our ancestors." Babila says, "Bakweri ancestors, velimo (translated as devils in English), act as mediators between the living and Maek'a Lowhe, the High God. They are contacted through divinations, during

[27] *Crampton and Bacon, Worldview, 4*
[28] *Mutia, Cahiers D'Etudes Africaines, 2–3*

libations, in dreams, visions, and during quiet moments of meditation."[29]

At the core of any unified set of people or society is a worldview that supports their way of reasoning and guides their actions. The truth is that no system or society in the world can survive without a unified system of thoughts and ideas. You don't need more than a week in Switzerland to know the Swiss people enjoy their high standards of life. So, they value hard work to buy items of top quality. Some fans would prefer a prison sentence than miss the Rio de Janeiro Carnival, the biggest in the world, which brings together over two million people, held annually since 1723.

Underneath these values and beliefs people hold is a quest for internal satisfaction. Unfortunately for many, including the Bakweries and carnival pilgrims, the entire journey is a gasping for the wind—time wasted on vanity. They have manufactured a god of their own who can't fill that gap. So, they become involved in diverse activities, waste their resources, and die without finding the meaning of the life for which they toiled night and day. One principal reason they fail to find a satisfactory meaning to life's schemes is their poor approach. What sense does it make to have devils mediating between you and God? What is there in a

---

[29] *Mutia, Cahiers D'Etudes Africaines, 4*

carnival of nudity that nourishes your soul with authentic knowledge?

Solomon warns in Proverbs 14:12, "There is a way that seems right to a man, but its end is the way of death." In his letter to the Colossian church, Paul warns, "Beware lest anyone cheat you though philosophy and empty deceit, according to the tradition of men, according to the basic principles of the world, and not according to Christ" (Colossians 2:8). Paul distinguishes between a good and bad philosophy. Those on the wrong path hold on to human traditions and things of this world. But those who focus on Jesus are in the right way, "For in Him dwells all the fullest of the Godhead bodily; and you are complete in Him, who is the head of all principality and power" (Colossians 2:9–10).

## THEOLOGICAL APPROACHES

How do people construct theologies? How do they put ideas together to create a belief system? These are essential questions we need to answer. Many factors influence a group of people to reason the way they do and act in ways different from others. The cultural setting is one of them. It shapes us and the way we think.

When we were younger, I used to believe *timbanabusa*, our traditional dish, was the most delicious in the world. My tribe's people live in the foothills of Mount Cameroon, the heart of the equatorial rain forest, a place where the cocoyam tuber and forest spices used to prepare *timbanabusa* flourish. But I developed some doubts about my position when I tasted *mbongo tchobi*, a delicious fish soup from the Douala community, a nearby tribe to ours.

In fact, I marveled in Dakar, the Senegalese capital, when I ate *cheebu jen*, made from a recipe of rice, various vegetables and spices. Later on in life, I ate the Indian lamb madras soup with rice, Thai green and red curry, and the famous Mexican wraps. I still can't decide what's the most delicious of all meals I have eaten. But I noticed one thing—everyone believes their traditional dish is the most delicious. That's normal because it is what you learn from childhood in your community. You get challenged only when you come out of your system of beliefs. Little did I know the Senegalese cannot grow cocoyam tubers as we do in Cameroon because of their geographical location.

I have understood we can only use what we have as resources to make life better for us. So, we interpret life based on what we know. Hence, the importance of having a philosophy that transcends cultures and traditions.

Another thing that affects the way people construct their theology is the environmental setting. Again, let me use my village as an example. We have at least eight to nine months of rainfall every year. To this day, most people in my village still depend on rainwater. Debundscha, one of the five wettest places on earth, with an estimated 10,299mm average annual rainfall, is in our region. It's obvious the most common color you notice there is green.

I was shocked when I arrived in the Republic of Mali in 2003. Worse, when I traveled across the desert regions between Mauritania and Morocco. *How can people and cattle survive here?* I asked myself. Of course, I'm used to harvesting fruits, veggies, tubers, and spices around the compound and backyards in my homeland. In these countries, however, sand covers sixty percent of the surface area. Most of what you see is brown, with only a few green spots across hundreds of miles.

A spirit of disbelief invaded me when I reached Kiruna, a town in the far north of Sweden. "May the Lord help me!" I exclaimed. Yes, for the first time in my life, I experienced temperatures as low as minus 40 degrees centigrade. I would never imagine conditions of that nature back home. We studied these things in geography lessons, but that was theory. To witness them for oneself is another reality.

People in these diverse geographical locations think and act differently based on their environmental conditions. Back in Mali and many west African countries, the people wear shorts, t-shirts, and boubous. May God have mercy on you if you try that during winter in Kiruna. The people of Kiruna make the most of their brief summer with a Summerfest and outdoor parties. In West and Central Africa, parties are all year round. The environment even affects the way people construct houses and various infrastructures. While every desert or forest inhabitant in interior Africa dreams of owning a four-wheel-drive vehicle, those in Europe want a Ferrari.

Those who grow up in Muslim-dominated places think and act differently from those with Christian, Buddhist, and pagan-dominated worldviews. You probably heard these statements: "I was born a Muslim," "I was born a Christian," or "I was born a traditional healer." Sometimes, a rare natural resource of value shapes the people's thinking in that community. With time, the resource shapes the way people trade and relate to the outside world. Many streets, villages, and even towns are named after a certain resource of value present there, an important infrastructure or a famous historical or talented person who contributed to making the place known to the outside world.

It goes on and on. It is not possible to mention all the factors that influence people to develop their beliefs and act the way they do. But remember, people want to make meaning out of life and find fulfillment. From an intellectual point of view, however, we can identify four ways we develop theologies:

The first is through an inductive approach. The one who reasons inductively goes "from a part to a whole, from particulars to generals, or from the individual to the universal."[30] As said earlier, from a single resource in the village, the people connect and trade with the outside world and make themselves known. From a core message in a single verse, we can generate practical life principles and solutions to confront our challenges. The Bible does not reject this way of reasoning. For instance, the wise man says, "Go to the ant, you sluggard! Consider her ways and be wise" (Proverbs 6:6). He tells us in this verse to examine the way ants behave. If we do that with diligence, we will generate a series of concepts that will help us in our own life endeavors. In the book, *Love & Respect* (Thomas Nelson, 2004), Dr. Emerson Eggerichs lives from a passage in the Bible, Ephesians 5:22-33, to come up with a concept he uses as a therapy to heal many sick marriages.

The second approach is the deductive way. Here, one gathers pieces of information, analyzes them diligently, and extracts pieces of evidence to prove a big topic. This manner of reasoning follows an investigative pattern. Detectives use it a lot to prove crimes. The Bible doesn't reject this way of arriving at truth. Christians involved in apologetics often use this approach. For instance, the Bible teaches, "By humility

---

[30] *Murrell, Systematic Theology, 22*

and the fear of the Lord are riches and honor and life."
How do we prove this statement is true? We go to the
Bible and collect verses that show humility and
honoring God come before riches. We also gather
stories of people in the Bible that show this concept.
Good examples are King Jehoshaphat, Hezekiah,
David, and Abraham. If we do a good job analyzing the
Bible passages, we show, "By humility and the fear of
the Lord are riches and honor and life" (Proverbs 22:4).
We can write a book on this subject, deliver many from
pride, and bless countless people. Christians use this
approach to refute false religions and logical fallacies
such as Islam, the theory of evolution, and atheism.

The third approach to developing theologies is through
speculation. Here, we assume a position based on
certain things we observe and then develop everything
else based on what we say in the assumption. Because
we don't know everything in life, we can assume certain
things, but thorough research must accompany this
assumption. The pieces of evidence we find in the field
either disprove or establish the assumption. Therefore,
one rule makes this approach authentic—back down if
you have no evidence or if your evidence is weak.

Here comes the problem: Humans are full of pride.
They don't like to back down. For instance:

> "Deism assumes the philosophical principle
> that God operates only according to natural
> law. Pantheism says that God is all; all is God.

Rationalism contends that the mind of man has created God, while evolution takes the position that man is a product of time + space + chance."[31]

Adherents of these belief systems have not produced sufficient evidence to prove their position. Have they backed down? No, they continue to teach their false doctrines. Only Christians can show you sufficient pieces of evidence to support their premise, "God exists and created us in His image." While we can speculate to enable research, we must stay objective and learn to spot and refute the insufficiencies of human doctrines.

The fourth and last way to build a theology is through mysticism. Here, people claim a special revelation from God. Often, those revelations are above Scripture. You may not question them when you accept them or belong to the system that claims them.

This is a dangerous approach. It often leads to error and destroys one's life. The Bible is against this way of reasoning. Almost every cult out there claims a special revelation from God. The *Book of Mormon* and its adherents made false predictions throughout history. Jehovah's Witnesses have even rewritten the Bible to suit their own beliefs. The occultists terrorize their

---

[31] *Murrell, Systematic Theology, 21*

followers with fear. Almost all charlatans I know follow strict rules and regulations. My uncle didn't allow anyone to cross with fire behind his back. He always sat and leaned on the wall to avoid that. I heard he was never supposed to put his hand under the bed, either. Have we not heard true stories of virgin and albino sacrifices to foreign gods, people who drink human and animal blood to please the gods? All these are baseless mystical beliefs that do not represent the true God of Abraham, Isaac, and Jacob. They prosper through fear and mind manipulation.

## TYPES OF THEOLOGY

Let's be sincere. Humans constantly increase their knowledge. Theology is vast. We can't limit it. In our booming technological era, knowledge is as precious as diamond. Just a few weeks ago, my pastor introduced me to the partial preterist view of eschatology (the study of the future) he embraces. I am used to the pre- , mid- and post-tribulation debates on the subject. Since I started studying theology in 2011, I never heard of the full or partial preterist views. A simple Google research informed me the view has been there for decades. In my few humble years of study, especially because I study on a part-time basis and principally for personal research and spiritual growth, I know I can't be exposed to all the theological views out there. None would master all in a lifetime but we can group them into five main types:

First, we have natural theology. The 1689 *Baptist Confession of Faith*, referenced by Stanford E. Murrell, ThD, defines natural theology as a "system of belief which appeals to objective facts contained in the works of God as distinct from the written revelation of Scripture."[32] In simple language, we look for information in nature that reveals God. Some things in nature are just "wow." The oceans, cliffs, forests, and cloud color patterns fascinate.

A friend of mine in Holland told me of the northern lights, a natural light display in the sky, predominantly seen in high-latitude regions. Although I was in Scandinavia, where these occur frequently in winter, I wasn't aware of them and never had the chance to witness them myself. But when I saw pictures on Google, they were wow. Such natural phenomena reveal God's majesty. There is no doubt about that.

Only, there are limitations to this natural approach to knowing God. The theologian observes nature and tries to find God through it. The fact is, this approach "tells of no way of pardon and peace with God, provides no escape from sin and its consequence, offers no way of eternal salvation, provides no incentive to holiness, and contains no sure revelation

---

[32] *Murrell, Systematic Theology, 22*

of the future."[33] Stanford adds, "Natural theology leaves man in the hands of impersonal laws which are believed to be irrevocable, irreversible, and impersonal."[34] This confirms David Clark's statement, "It is the testimony of time that the world has never been made better, nor humanity uplifted, by a purely natural religion."[35]

So, the search for God in nature has limitations because we cannot discover God sufficiently by ourselves without Him revealing Himself to us. In their efforts to find God in nature, some became idol worshippers of the sun, moon, stones and stars and developed doctrines of demons.

This brings us to the second type of theology, revealed theology, also known as biblical theology. Here, God seeks humans. He shows this when He writes the Bible and gives it to us. We can read the Bible's content to gain sufficient knowledge about Him. God revealed so many things in the Bible a lifetime cannot explore. But the Bible's core message doesn't change. It points to Jesus, the Messiah, who takes away the sins of humanity and makes a way to reunite in eternal fellowship with God. Every other exploration we make in life builds on this foundation.

[33] *Murrell, Systematic Theology, 23*

[34] *Murrell, Systematic Theology, 23*

[35] *Clark, Natural Theology, 23*

The third is practical theology. As the name implies, it refers to the "effect of divine truth upon the lives of professing Christians."[36] Here, we simply want to see whether those who call themselves Christians actually do the things God asks them to do. It is a way of not only hearing God's Word or divine truths but actually living it in one's life. We can find most practical theologies in the letters the apostles write to the churches. There, we discover all the topics we need in our daily interactions with others and in the world.

The fourth type of theology is dogmatic. It concentrates on the core doctrines of the church. These doctrines are the virgin birth and sinless life of Jesus, His substitutionary death, resurrection from the dead, the second coming, our preparation to be with Him, evangelism, and more. These are the foundations of any gospel we preach. We have a mission to stick to these core doctrines, remind ourselves of them, and not deviate from them. The early Church didn't compromise these doctrines, as one sees in Acts 2:42, "And they continued steadfastly in the apostles' doctrine and fellowship, in the breaking of bread, and in prayers."

The fifth and last type of theology is theology proper. God is not the product of our imaginations. He reveals Himself to us. Because He does so, we want to know

[36] *Murrell, Systematic Theology, 24*

Him. Hence, theology proper refers to the efforts we put in to understand who God is. In the Bible's sense, we want to build a personal relationship with Him, not just have some carnal knowledge of who He is. We want to experience Him in life, as says Paul, "that I may know Him and the power of His resurrection, and the fellowship of His sufferings, being conformed to His death..." (see Philippians 3:10). How do we know we know Him? When everything He says reflects in us, we see Him through His Word. We are part of Him; He is part of us. Writing to the Colossians, Paul articulates this well; "Set your mind on things above, not on things on the earth. For you died, and your life is hidden with Christ in God. When Christ who is our life appears, then you also will appear with Him in glory" (Colossians 3:2-4).

## BRANCHES OF THEOLOGY PART ONE

Where do we begin? It will take years to go through all that is out there in the name of theology. In fact, a simple internet search takes you to all kinds of information. There's no limit to the explorations of theological concepts. All we can do in this section is try to group those parts of theology that are relevant to this study. Again, as you go through these few branches of theology, we mention here, try to analyze how they differ or are similar to the Bible's content.

The first branch of theology we want to explore is systematic theology. As the word implies, this is a standardized attempt to organize God's revelations in the Bible in a set of doctrinal parts. Each of these parts is an entire field of exploration. What systematic theology does is lay the foundation for further exploration according to Scripture. Most Christian institutions organize their systematic theology in different ways, but systematic theology typically comprises six parts.

The first is theology proper or the study of God, as we already saw above. In theology proper, we ask if God even exists. How do we prove His existence? We explore God's nature, His decrees and works, and gather all pieces of evidence about Him. Then, we present this information to the entire Christian community and unbelievers on diverse platforms. You can't engage in a debate with an atheist, evolutionist, or Islamist if you don't have a thorough knowledge of theology proper.

The second part of systematic theology is bibliology, the study of the Bible. What is inside the Bible? What makes its content authentic? How can you be sure Scripture comes from God? What pieces of evidence are there? Here, we make use of apologetics, another branch of theology we will explore later. With the use of apologetic tools, we explore topics under bibliology such as biblical inerrancy, the belief the Bible has no errors or mistakes in its teachings, inspiration of the Scriptures, external pieces of evidence to support biblical claims such as the Dead Sea Scrolls, language translation, church fathers, and so on.

Anthropology is the third part of systematic theology. It is the study of the human being. Here, we explore what a human being comprises: whether we are made of a body and spirit or a body, spirit, and soul. We analyze the human being's original state in the Garden of Eden, what happened when Adam and Eve sinned against God, and how sin affects humanity today.

This part of systematic theology also explores how God interacts with humans. It examines why human beings need a savior to deliver them from sin. Also, we compare the human beings God created with those the theory of evolution claims evolved from nothing. Anthropology analyzes all other definitions and studies of the human being in other religions and worldviews. With the help of reason and revelation, it exposes all fallacies or insufficiencies in their definitions of what human beings are.

Soteriology is the fourth part of systematic theology, and it is the study of salvation. Most Bible-based Christian theologians would agree on the first three parts, with minor variations in their definitions. But for the study of salvation, we notice significant contradictions. Some believe salvation is by works. Others say it is by grace alone through faith in Jesus.

Then, we have the famous debate between predestination and freewill. For hundreds of years, Calvinists and Arminians have knocked each other really hard from their own sides of this debate.

Of course, if you read your Bible well, you discover salvation is by grace alone though faith in Jesus the Messiah. Yet, true salvation is clearly evident in works. The Bible doesn't talk about faith and neglect works; it encourages us to balance them. James clearly expounds on this subject. Don't talk about faith if you have no works. If you profess to know Christ and are His disciple, what should be your logical reaction? Make it clear so the world can see, right? What pattern do you see in the life of Jesus, His apostles, and early Christians? Don't some even die for their faith? This, of course, doesn't mean salvation is by works, which is a heresy.

Oh, maybe we are not on the same page right now. This book is not an argument about how one gets saved. The paragraph above simply exposes some polemics in the study of salvation. He who talks about salvation can't ignore Jesus. So, soteriology studies the historical background of redemption, God's sovereignty, and the atonement. It also analyzes how other religions see Jesus the Messiah and exposes all the logical fallacies in them.

The fifth part of systematic theology is pneumatology, the study of the Holy Spirit. Jesus made a big promise when He was about to physically leave the world. "Nevertheless, I tell you the truth. It is to your advantage that I go away; for if I do not go away, the Helper will not come to you; but if I depart, I will send Him to you" (John 16:7). We know He fulfilled this promise in Acts 2 when the Holy Spirit invaded the believers on the Day of Pentecost. Since then, He, the Holy Spirit, has been in the world, helping us to do God's will and advance His kingdom.

Soteriology looks at everything concerning the characteristics, nature and works of the Holy Spirit, and how the world resists His works. It looks at the role of grace, what happens when one gets saved, baptism, justification before God, and a holy lifestyle. Here also, we explore the safety and security of the saints and how sin affects our salvation. Then, we study the concept of salvation in other religions and fallacies within the fake Christian cycles, such as Christian cults, secular cults, satanism, and the occult.

The sixth and last part of systematic theology we consider is eschatology, the study of the future. No area of theological studies causes divisions among Christians other than eschatology. Sadly, the division is so great it sometimes leads to hatred. In eschatology, we want to know what happens to us when we die. We also explore prophecies and Christ's second coming, the events of the end of times and the rapture of the saints, Heaven, the eternal home of the saints, and Hell, the eternal home of those who reject Jesus. We look into the war of Armageddon and the one-thousand-year reign of Jesus on earth. We explore false concepts about end-time events in other worldviews and focus on the Bible to protect our faith from harmful beliefs.

To these six branches of systematic theology, you can also add angelology, the study of angels; Christology, the study of Jesus the Christ; ecclesiology, the doctrine of the church, and hamartiology, the study of sin.

## BRANCHES OF THEOLOGY PART TWO

Systematic theology touches almost everything. It is a good idea for Bible students to begin their study of theology with it to introduce themselves to most of the fields of theology. Systematic theology doesn't get too much into the nitty gritty of every topic, but it gives you a well-informed definition of the branches of theology, although some variations exist among individual theological systems of belief.

Let's look at Christian apologetics. We derive the English word "apologetics" from the Greek word *apologia*, which means make a defense. "Apologetics is that branch of Christian theology that answers the question "Is the Christian faith believable?"[37]

---

[37] *Dr. Saneesh and Dr. Johnson, Integrated Apologetics, 1*

The Christian faith suffers many attacks from skeptics, other religions, and worldviews.

> "The last four to five centuries have been a time in history when anti-Christian philosophies and thought patterns have flourished to the full extent in Christian societies. Humanism, a philosophy in which man has been elevated to the position of God, is the philosophy of the present times. It is the foundation of almost all the present-day ways of thinking and education."[38]

Apologetics is simply a defense of the Christian faith. The Bible in 1 Peter 3:15 motivates us to engage in apologetics, "But sanctify the Lord God in your hearts, and always be ready to give a defense to everyone who asks you a reason for the hope that is in you, with meekness and fear." All Christians should engage in some form of apologetics. If you claim to know Jesus, the world will attack your faith in Him; you should be ready to give an answer to anyone who questions your beliefs.

The purpose of Christian apologetics is:

> "…to refute all the accusations that are brought against the Bible and the Christian faith. Show only the Bible and the Christian way of life

[38] *Dr. Saneesh and Dr. Johnson, Integrated Apologetics, 1*

work in actual life and that only the Bible and the Christian faith provide permanent peace and happiness. Remove the sincere doubts in the hearts of believers and unbelievers so that we eliminate the hindrances of their spiritual growth. To provide sufficient evidence to those who attack the Christian faith."[39]

The branches of Christian apologetics are many. It depends on who attacks the Christian faith and what area of our faith they attack. If they attack the very foundation on which the Christian faith founds itself, we better know the foundation on which the one who attacks us stand. Hence, we enter a branch of apologetics called pre-suppositional apologetics. "Presuppositions are the starting truths upon which we build different fields of knowledge and investigations, the basic and starting assumptions upon which we build the rest of the subject."[40]

In pre-suppositional apologetics, we study the foundational beliefs of the worldview that attack us and expose the fallacies in them. This is an excellent way to refute cults such as Mormons, Jehovah's Witnesses, Moonies, Christian Science Church, Church of Scientology, Children of God movement, Worldwide Church of God, Spiritualism, Church Universal and Triumphant, Unitarianism, Universalism, Gnosticism,

[39] *Dr. Saneesh and Dr. Johnson, Integrated Apologetics, 10*
[40] *Dr. Saneesh and Dr. Johnson, Presuppositions, 1*

Neo-Gnosticism, Way International, Holy Order of MANS, and the Church of the Living God.

Through pre-suppositional apologetics, we also refute New Age groups such as monism, pantheism, panentheism, reincarnation, Karma, personal transformation, ecological responsibility groups, and universal religions. Pre-suppositional apologetics also serves as a tool to refute secular cults and humanist groups such as Christian humanism, cultural humanism, literary humanism, modern humanism, philosophical humanism, Renaissance humanism, religious humanism, and secular humanism.

In fact, you won't believe all of these groups exist out there. The ones named here do not even make up one percent of the false religions you can find. Pre-suppositional apologetics help us understand what each of these movements holds as beliefs. You don't need to study all of Islam, Buddhism, demonic traditions, science only, and evolution to refute their claims. This part of apologetics focuses on the foundation on which they lay their entire doctrines. We show them how weak the foundation is upon which they build their entire life. Then, we present them with pieces of evidence in support of the authenticity of the Christian faith to help them come to the knowledge of the truth in Jesus.

While pre-suppositional apologetics focuses on the foundational beliefs of worldviews, philosophical apologetics goes a step further into some details of their doctrines. We want to expose not only the errors in the foundations on which they built their doctrines but also the errors in reasoning. Philosophical apologetics comes in to facilitate the process. It separates the worldviews into various philosophical groups, notably theistic, atheistic, occult, and non-theistic philosophies.

Sometimes, the opposition uses archaeological discovers and science to attack the Christian faith. In the last century, Christians developed a branch called historical or legal apologetics to deal with claims in the field of science and archaeology. Here, the Christian apologist looks into subjects such as the Bible and history, the Bible and archaeology, the Bible and prophecies, the Bible and linguistics, and so on. The principal objective of this branch of apologetics is to find evidence to support the Bible and the Christian faith. So, we adopt the investigative reconstruction and legal methods, where we define and show proof. We use tools such as archaeology, dating techniques, linguistic studies, status of the Bible manuscripts, history and chronology, culture, customs and manners over the years, language meanings, historical incidents, and text transmission. We clarify the type of proof or truth using tools such as axiomatic truth, logical proof, mathematical proof, empirical proof, historical-legal proof, model-based proof, and relational proof.

Another branch of apologetics, known as rational or scientific apologetics, focuses on refuting the claim that modern science is the way forward for humanity. Many people believe everything that comes from the field of science is truth. More people trust artificial intelligence more than their own reasoning process. Science has become the god they worship. Rational or scientific apologetics gets into the details of the claims of science, especially in the theory of evolution, to disprove their claims. Here, we also look at subjects such as Bible difficulties, Bible and science, Bible and evolution, Bible and astronomy, and cosmogony. We explain the reliability of the canon (Bible), expose its inerrancy, and why we trust it as the reliable source of absolute truth. We differentiate between normative, physical, biological, historical, and sociological sciences. We look into the roles qualitative and quantitative models play in exposing scientific truths and their limits on genuine scientific explorations.

You may say, "We can't go any deeper than what we saw so far." But in apologetics, we're still exploring the tip of the iceberg. We can go as far as analyzing human thinking and motives. Hence, we enter another field of apologetics called propaganda analysis and mind manipulation techniques. This field of apologetics looks into logic and logical fallacies in human thinking—manipulative propaganda.

For our benefit, we first analyze difficulties that arise in the Christian faith, such as errors of interpretation, Scripture twisting, and Bible difficulties. Bible difficulties include subjects such as difficulties arising from the original text, translation problems, false interpretation of the Bible, wrong conceptions of the Bible, language in which the Bible was originally written, incomplete knowledge of Bible times customs, history, geography, and society of Bible times. We look into our ignorance of the condition under which a certain Bible book was written, why God gave us certain commands, the limitations of a human being's understanding, the nature of Bible statements, and the significance of numbers in the Bible.

Once we have enough knowledge of these, we can confidently analyze the scientific information we encounter in false systems of beliefs. We expose the logical fallacies people who attack the Christian faith use and the propaganda and mind manipulation techniques they adopt. We look into their prejudice and bias, meaning, and perception of things.

We use four action filters: forbidden, tolerable, desirable, and essential actions. Once we know the category in which they fall, we draw the barriers in human reasoning based on the Scriptures, expose the extent to which their values changed or shifted from right to wrong, and show them their ethical responsibility to rely on truth by renouncing sinful choices. One way to do this is to engage them in structured debates and leading questions.

Every topic we mentioned under Christian apologetics is an area of specialization. It is difficult for a single individual to master all these branches. You can specialize in refuting and bringing Muslims to the knowledge of the truth in Jesus or in evangelizing Christian cults and occult movements such as Freemasons. Maybe you want to go public on debate platforms to engage with atheists, evolutionists, and science-only adherents. The truth is that you have to specialize in one or a few areas to be effective in your mission.

## BRANCHES OF THEOLOGY PART THREE

Part Two focused mostly on Christian apologetics. Of course, not everyone is in a direct defense of the Christian faith on social platforms or positions of leadership. God called some of us to pastor churches and take care of His flock. Here, we study the books of the Bible, their history, when the writers wrote them, the conditions under which they wrote, and the core messages in their books. The objective is to make the most use of Bible books and rightly divide the Word of Truth.

However, we don't limit ourselves to the study of Bible books, even if it is the core exercise of every theologian.

We also read excellent Christian materials and thoughts from writers on specific topics such as church planting, church development, ethics, evangelism, good, evil, suffering, Godly love, the life of Jesus, children ministry, family ministry, leadership, spiritual growth, discipleship, entrepreneurship, discipline, reason and faith, Christian psychology, morality, prayer, kingdom values, holiness, practical Christian lifestyle, faith issues, doing business as a Christian, and more.

Depending on what God called us to do and the audience we have to reach, we engage in Bible study and read Christian inspirational research materials that help us meet that need. Maybe God wants us to reach out to children in a community, do charity in a region, target specific habits and traditions in society, build an internet platform, engage in a targeted education, etc. It all depends on your calling. If you deal with many ethnic groups, study Christian sociology to help you move along. As a college evangelist, make sure you understand the things in our modern world college students struggle with and get rooted before confronting them.

Now that we have a thorough background of theology, let's look into the reasons God allows theological studies.

Chapter Three

# REASONS GOD
# ALLOWS THEOLOGY

W e've got the Bible God Himself wrote. Why do we need theology? Why should we engage in theological studies? Can't we just read the Bible? Are we not creating confusion? Yes, these questions are pertinent, and we should look at them carefully.

Let's consider the famous Mount Cameroon, the highest peak in West and Central Africa. Earlier, I said our village is on the foothills of this gigantic pile of materials. We'll assume you have a research mission to study this mountain and write a book about it based on evidence. The first thing you do is travel there to see it for yourself.

In a couple of weeks, you walk through every part of the mountain and observe the rocks, caves, vegetation, and animals living on it. You even collect samples of materials to analyze in the lab to know the type of rocks and ground the mountain is made of. You analyze the topology and climate conditions, too. All of these form the visible information you can collect about the mountain.

Yet, there is much more about the mountain you can't easily see. You hear from eyewitnesses that some parts of the mountain have gold and precious minerals. You wonder about this information. Doesn't an active volcanic mountain consist mostly of rocks? But you don't have the equipment or expertise to verify this information. You engage a private firm that checks whether some sections of the mountain have precious minerals underneath. The firm performs a series of experiments and gives you the results.

You hear the villagers say the Germans fought World War II on parts of this mountain and you want to confirm the authenticity of that claim. So, you arrange meetings with some of the oldest people in the village and surrounding villages. They tell you how these things happened. Some even take you to a specific location where villagers claim soldiers dug a mass grave and buried those who died in the war. How can you stay indifferent to this information? You hire the services of a specialized archaeological agency. They conduct experiments and discover human skulls and bones in that location. Another firm specialized in analyzing plants and animal remains performs experiments on these discoveries and the location and confirms they were actually German soldiers who died during the war.

Still, your research doesn't end there. You want to know how many eruptions occurred on this mountain and the damages they caused. So, you contact specialized offices of the local administration that have archives of this information. You learn about the first documented eruption of the mountain, the recent ones, and how the government and the people reacted. You also learn about the damage to the plants and animal species on the mountain and in surrounding regions.

Yet, your research continues because the villagers tell you they performed special ancestral practices on the mountain. You learn each village has its own set of traditions and rituals. So, you move from village to village to gather this information. Many confirm the god of the mountain is called *efasa moto*, translated as half-human. They narrate the tales of this god and the impact on the lives of the people. You also hear the villagers say their ancestors sacrificed animals, virgin girls, and albinos to appease this god. You try to confirm this information, but you find no reliable person to talk to. You later discover most of those extremely wicked practices were real but didn't survive to this day because many in the younger generations embraced the Christian faith. So, you go further to study the linguistic, cultural, and traditional developments. Finally, you organize all the information you gathered.

Of course, there is much more you can do; there's a lot more information you can collect. We know total knowledge is not possible. In every field of science, we deal with sufficient knowledge. You have sufficient knowledge at hand to write a comprehensive and well-informed book about Mount Cameroon based on evidence. Anyone who reads the book sees the pictures in the book, learns about the history of its volcanic activity, knows what one can find underneath, understands the traditions of those who live on the foothills of the mountain, and how the mountain shapes the mentality of the people.

Notice one thing: There are things about the mountain you can discover on your own during the research. For others, you need the help of some specialists. For things like traditions and historical events on the mountain, you can't know by observing the mountain. The villagers give you hints. You conduct experiments or investigations to find evidence to establish or refute their claims.

So, sometimes, the mountain itself does not give you sufficient information about some aspects of itself. You need some help from entities outside the mountain. A similar observation goes to the Bible.

When we read the Bible, we don't easily recognize areas where interpretation challenges may arise because of our lack of knowledge of the language and culture of Bible times, but the apologetics field of linguistics and archaeology can help bring more light to the subject. The Bible doesn't explain how it was compiled into 66 books, chapters, and verses. Why these 66 books and not the other books we know as non-canonical? The field of bibliology helps us get into the details of its composition with external pieces of evidence.

The Bible doesn't mention many of our church fathers, who fought hard to preserve the Bible we have today. Wouldn't you like to know what happened behind the scenes? The study of the historicity of the Bible serves that purpose. It can help to either strengthen your faith or expose weaknesses in other worldviews.

From what we have said so far, have you been able to identify some reasons why God allows theological studies? Let's expose some of them.

## WE ARE KNOWLEDGE HUNTERS

The first reason is that we want to expand our knowledge of God and the Bible. The more we know about the Bible and God, even with external pieces of evidence, the more we establish our faith in Him and in His Word. We notice the Bible gives us strong hints but doesn't spell out the foundational beliefs of cultists, occultists, evolutionists, and Muslims. With the help of those hints in the Bible, Christian apologists organize this information in pre-suppositional apologetics. Today, we understand what every one of these belief systems holds on to. It becomes easier to refute their claims and present them solid evidence in favor of the Christian faith.

Do you remember how the Mount Cameroon researcher discovered valuable information about the mountain from outside sources, even though his major focus was the mountain? We know so many things about the Bible happened behind the scenes. These things increase our knowledge of events in Bible times. For instance, no book faced more criticism in the world's history than the Bible. One may think the discovery of fossil fuels helps the theory of evolution. Rather, it is primary evidence there was a great flood in the days of Noah.

Therefore, we engage in theological explorations because we want to gain critical knowledge that supports biblical claims. This knowledge helps us to confront critics and present a more authentic gospel to sincere inquires.

## WE ARE TREASURE HUNTERS

The second reason we want to expand our knowledge of God is that He hid treasures in His Word, and we want to discover them. Sometimes, He gathers them in one spot. Other times, He scatters them all over the place, requiring diligence and patience to unfold them.

Let's take the example of the world we live in and its treasures. In recent years, researchers discovered enormous reserves of cobalt, copper, tellurium, manganese, lithium, and other valuable resources that contribute to making technology better. Without tremendous investments in technological research and innovation, we would not enjoy the services of things like smartphones and better means of transportation. We can't discover these treasures unless we explore.

The Bible is our internal spiritual mine field. The world and the entire universe are the external mine fields. All Christian researchers and Bible students are the explorers of the internal and external pieces of evidence in these fields. The mining instrument we use is theology. With it, we dig across every part of the Bible, world, and universe to discover its hidden treasures. We make the treasures available for everyone to exploit and improve his or her spiritual life. Look into the Christian book market. We find amazing books about marriage, business, family, raising children, holiness, missions, etc. Don't we all get help from some of these materials we consume? All these are the hidden treasures in the Bible unfolded.

## WE SEEK GOD'S WAY

Christians know God created everything visible and invisible for a purpose. Many times, God reminds us He has a plan for our lives and extends His hands to us with an invitation to seek His face so He guides us into fulfilling it. We also know we live in a fallen world, one that constantly wages war against us and our relationship with Him. Often, the world distracts us and catches us in its own futilities and craftiness.

Therefore, theological reflections become central to all aspects of our lives. One reason theology is so important is that advanced by Vincent Cheung, ... "it deals with the verbal revelation that comes from the supreme being—the essential reality that gives existence and meaning to everything."[41] Our mission on earth is to know the Father, His will for us, and to do it. We want to find a divine interpretation of all our endeavors. The world has its own interpretations of life and the things we see. "But ignorance of divine revelation," says Cheung, "affects all of thought and life, from one's view toward history and philosophy to one's interpretation of music and literature, to one's understanding of mathematics and physics."[42]

[41] *Cheung, Theology, 9*
[42] *Cheung, Theology, 10*

There is a way God wants us to approach every situation in life. God has His own definition for everything. We don't want to be ignorant of His approaches to life. So, we engage in theological studies to discover those priceless divine patterns that bring not only meaning to our lives but also glory to God.

## ORGANIZATION AND EFFICIENCY

A few months ago, I wanted to offer a friend an English grammar book to improve his English language skills. I went to the city bookstore to buy one. At the store's entrance, I saw a board on which was a map of how they organized the entire bookshop. From the board, I learned the language books were on the second floor, on the left wall. To be more specific, the books in English were on the right edge of that wall. I walked straight there. It took me only about five minutes to find a book for him.

Imagine if the bookstore had no directories. The bookstore keepers merely put books on any empty shelves they find. A customer comes in and wants to buy a history book. Where does one find the book? You may research the entire shop and not find what you are looking for. But when we create a place for everything and make sure everything is in its space, even the shopkeeper finds pleasure in directing people to the right spots.

We earlier saw God scattered treasures all over the place in the Bible. Theology helps us not only to gather many of these treasures but also to organize them according to their kinds. Today, when we confront a Christian cult, all we do is go to pre-suppositional apologetics, learn about the cult's foundational beliefs, and develop a strategy to refute their claims. If evolutionists make noise, we guide them to the scientific evidence for design, creation, and the flood in Noah's days to generate irrefutable arguments against them. In every field of thought, theologians generated materials and pieces of evidence to support the Christian faith. These help us be effective in bringing every thought into captivity to the knowledge of Christ.

## NO BORING LIFE

Let's come back to the research on Mount Cameroon. The researcher publishes a book about the mountain, returns to his own land, and makes a few thousand dollars. As a child born in a village in the mountain's foothills, you buy a copy of this book out of curiosity or to increase your knowledge of the mountain. In the book, you see amazing photos of cliffs, volcanic craters, rocks, and thick equatorial forests. You also discover the researcher adds pictures of rare wild animal species such as baboons, elephants, monkeys, antelopes, and many other creatures.

It doesn't end there. The researcher includes the reports of the companies that conducted research on the presence of rare minerals underneath some parts of the mountain. According to the historical pattern of volcanic activity in the area, an eruption is likely to occur after every 10 to 20 years. Soil samples reveal the mountain regions have one of the richest soil types on the planet, with plenty of annual rainfall. The lava remains are excellent for road construction.

In fact, the researcher says time didn't permit his team to write everything they discovered about the mountain; they left samples of these things yet to be analyzed with the local council authorities. Maybe they will find someone interested in going further with the research.

You read this book. As a child born in a village in the mountain's foothills, what do you do about it? People in your village complain of poverty. There's no drinking water; everyone depends on rainwater. There's water scarcity in the dry season. Crops don't yield well despite having rich soils. Most village youths migrate to already congested cities in search of greener pastures. Your village has no school or training center. You wake up every morning; the mountain looks at you; you look at it. You see and hear the same things every day. Is that how you continue to live your life, even with such information at hand? How dare you complain of poverty? Don't you have a brain?

Most people in the village know about the researcher and how he asked them questions during his research activities, but they are not interested in going any further than that. The government authorities put the research samples in their office drawers and forgot about them. What will you do?

Here comes the explorer. A book like that is a hidden treasure for the explorer. He or she wants to do something about it. He looks around and discovers no company extracts the minerals. The mountain has enough wood to build a school from kindergarten right up to a university, but no one thinks about that. The few local tourist agencies content themselves with walking to a few accessible places on the mountain, but the explorer imagines cable cars with stunning views. In fact, the explorer sees no limits to opportunities—already sees himself or herself as a millionaire.

The Bible and the world around are like the mountain with hidden treasures to exploit. Christians are explorers. Theology is the mining instrument we use to explore and extract the resources in their masses to benefit all. The greatest people we ever had on earth are those who engaged in theological explorations. Their discoveries continue to bless us to this day.

How stupid it is to live in one of those villages in the foothills of the mountain and cry of poverty with this research at hand! How ridiculous it is to read your Bible, dump it there, and do nothing about it! Oh no!

Muslims, Buddhists, atheists, cultists, traditionalists, your family, work colleagues, club friends; many of these people are not aware of the hidden treasures in the Bible. Jesus gave us a command to reach out to them. Therefore, God allows theological explorations for that purpose.

The explorer embarks on a tourist project in his village. He finds partners in Switzerland to build a cable car station for tourists to visit the mountain. He also constructs two amazing hotels and restaurants on the mountain in specific spots. He is the first to engage in such a project on a mountain in Central Africa. His idea exposes the village to the entire region and country. In a matter of months, people travel from nearby countries to the village. Most tourists who visit Cameroon want to visit the village and see the mountain.

In less than two years, the village is open to the entire world, with people coming from as far as Australia. Within this period, the standard of life of the villagers improved significantly. Most can find employment in their village. Village youths no longer think of traveling out of the village because the explorer's idea opened their eyes to other opportunities they could pursue.

In the same manner, when we use theology to explore the Bible and make use of its hidden treasures, not only do we bring glory to God, but also we improve our lives and the lives of others around us by bringing them from darkness to light. That is no boring lifestyle. Imagine a world in which you cannot explore. You know everything; there's nothing more to learn about. You wake up, eat, do some routine stuff, and sleep. Won't life bore you to death?

Theological explorations bring excitement in our lives because we have unending hope of laying hold of priceless treasures from the Bible at the end of every adventure.

Chapter Four

# SIMILARITIES BETWEEN
# THE BIBLE AND THEOLOGY

## GOD IS GLORIFIED

We unveiled some similarities between the Bible and theology in the previous chapters, but it benefits us more to spell them out clearly. There are five fundamental similarities. Let's dive deeply into them.

The first is they both glorify God, but on the condition that only God inspires the theology. As we have seen, there are theologies that the Holy Spirit inspires, and there are those He doesn't. God doesn't inspire the nonsense literature on Jehovah's Witnesses demoting Jesus to a mere human being. Neither did he inspire Joseph Smith's failed prophesies or his movement's polygamous practices. God doesn't tell people to start cults and engage in occult practices and witchcraft. He is not the inspirer of the theory of evolution, New Age groups, science only, and humanist theories. Whenever God inspires a theology, it brings glory to Him, just as the Bible does. Historical Legal Apologetics, for instance, uses archaeology and dating techniques to understand ancient civilizations. It goes beyond surface level and explores the importance of linguistic studies for the Bible. The added value is our improved ability to explain difficult passages in the Bible.

This leads to the second similarity between theology and the Bible.

## HOLY-SPIRIT-INSPIRED

The Holy Spirit inspired the Bible. He inspires good theology as well. The Bible tells us God inspired all Scriptures. God's Word has hidden treasures. Through meditation, the Holy Spirit helps us develop theologies that extract these treasures for use by all. None can interpret the Bible correctly without the Holy Spirit's help.

In the same way, no good theology is of human inspiration. The Bible says, "...the natural man does not receive the things of the Spirit of God, for they are foolishness to him; nor can he know them, because they are spiritually discerned" (1 Corinthians 2:14). As much as God inspired everything in the Bible, He is the One who also guides us to develop theologies that better explain His will for humankind. Our generations are blessed to have compiled materials from theological thinkers of many generations in history to learn from. The book you're currently reading is a great example.

## SALVATION ORIENTED

The third similarity between the Bible and theology is they both have a common objective. That objective is to show us the way to salvation, to become saved, to grow in faith, and to preach the gift of salvation to others. Earlier, we saw the entire Bible points to a common theme: Jesus the Messiah. The Old Testament prepares the way for Him. Jesus comes in the New Testament, re-establishes the lost relationship with God, and guides us into the new life in Him with the help of the Holy Spirit. Theology does nothing more than expand our knowledge of what Jesus accomplished on the cross.

Why do we spend sleepless nights doing archaeological, geological, and historical research? What motivates us to organize debates with Muslims, atheists, and those in other false religions? We can also sleep, eat, drink, marry, have children, and party every day. But we limit our engagement in these things because we want to represent Jesus on earth and preach the Good News to the lost so they can also be saved. God loves when we devote our lives to bringing others to the knowledge of the truth. Hence, Paul says, "…we make it our aim, whether present or absent, to be well pleasing to Him" (2 Corinthians 5:9).

## NOTHING BUT SERVANTS

The fourth similarity between the Bible and theology is that both produce servants. The wisdom of humans is so insignificant compared to what the Holy Spirit reveals in the Bible. Each time we read the Bible and meditate on its teachings, it challenges our intellect in various areas of our lives. The deeper we delve into God's Word, the stronger our craving for it becomes, revealing our need for more of God in our lives.

God's Word has a divine capacity to humble us because we know we cannot equate our human wisdom to it. The Holy Spirit testifies within us we are God's servants. So, we study the Bible daily and endeavor to serve God in every area of our lives. The reason for engaging in theological studies is that we want to grow spiritually, increase our knowledge of God and His ways, and improve our capacity to serve in a certain God-called ministry. There's no need to boast because we hold a theological degree. Instead, the more knowledge we gain, the more service God requires from us. Jesus says, "But he who is greatest among you shall be your servant" (Matthew 23:11). And "For everyone to whom much is given, from him much will be required; and to whom much has been committed, of him they will ask the more" (See Luke 12:48).

## SPIRITUAL GROWTH

The fifth and last similarity between the Bible and theology is they both help us grow spiritually. If God didn't give us the Bible and His Holy Spirit to guide us, it would be hard for us to understand His will for us. Then, God would need to appear to each one of us. If the Holy Spirit doesn't inspire good theologies, we would struggle with building a consistent Christian worldview.

Our hunger and desire to know more about God push us to study His Word. Second Timothy 2:15 says, "Be diligent to present yourself approved to God, a worker who does not need to be ashamed, rightly dividing the word of truth." We study and increase in knowledge because we know God wants to use us. The knowledge we gain from the Bible through meditation is excellent. Supporting this knowledge with pieces of evidence from the field of theology is wonderful. The result is that we put ourselves in a position where God can use us to bring glory to Himself and move the unsaved from darkness to light.

Our Father looks for people to whom He can commit important tasks of the kingdom project. His desire is that all His children be in a position where He can use them to win unbelievers into His kingdom. Knowledge helps us improve our spiritual capacities. It propels us to positions of leadership.

To lead in God's eyes is to have a bigger capacity to serve more people in your area of calling. A spiritually mature person handles complex things with ease. Knowledge helps the person to rightly divide the Word of Truth. The Bible says, "Wise people store up knowledge," You had better not put knowledge into a fool's hands. "...but the mouth of the foolish is near destruction" (Proverbs 10:14).

Chapter Five

# DIFFERENCES BETWEEN
# THE BIBLE AND THEOLOGY

## AUTHORITY

We can't say it enough. The Bible contains God's Word and His will for humanity. Theology is the method by which we seek and reason about God, His Word, and His will for humankind, organizing information and gathering evidence to understand Him better. To put things into perspective, the Bible lays the foundation for what we need to know about God and His will for us. Theology builds on that foundation to further explore those things about God and His will for us.

There are things the Bible says explicitly. For a few, we need outside sources to understand their meaning. Remember the research on Mount Cameroon; the mountain itself could not tell the researcher the history of volcanic activities. He went to the local offices to collect that information. He consulted a private firm to confirm minerals underneath some parts of the mountain. In the same way, theology explores and explains things about the Bible, the world, and the universe. But it does not take the place of the Bible; it brings more details to us about certain things the Bible doesn't.

## INSPIRATION

The Holy Spirit inspired everything in the Bible. Second Timothy 3:16 says, "...all Scripture is given by inspiration of God..." Not some parts of it, but all. Peter says, "...holy men of God spoke as they were moved by the Holy Spirit" (2 Peter 2:21). Paul adds in Romans 15:4, "For whatever things were written before were written for our learning, that we through the patience and comfort of the Scriptures might have hope." So, we know the Bible is God's message, but He does not inspire all theologies out there. Bias, subjectivity and prejudice are constant threats to human thoughts. Ask yourself why we have many divisions in the Christian community—bias contaminated our thinking process and infiltrated our theologies.

> The Bible says: ...with all lowliness and gentleness, with longsuffering, bearing with one another in love, endeavoring to keep the unity of the Spirit in the bond of peace. There

> is one body and one Spirit, just as you were
> called in one hope of your calling; one Lord,
> one faith, one baptism; one God and Father of
> all, who is above all, and through all, and in you
> all (Ephesians 4:2-5).

But what do we find out there? Some say they are Catholics, others apostolic. Still, many call themselves evangelicals, Presbyterians, full gospel, Episcopal, Orthodox, etc. It doesn't end there. One group identifies itself as Calvinists, the other Arminians, full or partial preterist. Many describe themselves as non-denominational, others interdenominational. Hence, we have Catholic, Presbyterian, apostolic, and Orthodox doctrines. Calvinists would not interpret some passages of Scripture the way Arminians do. We are all caught up in this confusion, even conflict.

The truth is that God does not inspire all these divisions. Unfortunately, most of us belong to one or more of these systems of belief. Some good news is, however, that all the polemics help to advance our research on Scriptures and increase our knowledge about God from diverse angles. This spiritual growth occurs only when we read our Bible, meditate on its content, and decide to let it guide us into theological explorations. God knows how to guide our steps to the truth amid chaos.

## AUTHENTICITY

The Bible's message is always trustworthy and true. Of course, the Holy Spirit inspired it. So, we read the Bible, knowing God Himself talks to us. There's no risk of wrongly believing and applying its content with the Holy Spirit's help. The only pain every true believer must experience for believing and living by what the Bible says is persecution.

Theology needs caution. It leads to the wrong direction when bias, subjectivity, and prejudice contaminate it. When that happens, it works to defend personal interests or self-defined values of a system of beliefs, that do not bring glory to God. Observe the way Arminians and Calvinists threw insults at each other over the years; we can't but lament for such an error. The sad part is how those arguments grew to hatred among some groups. The enemy used this self-made chaos to fight and weaken believers in some areas of their lives.

If the Bible tells us to move in unity, should we not give up our personal interests and join hands to look for the best way forward? When conflicts arose over circumcision between the Jewish and Gentile converts in Acts 15, what did the spiritual leaders of that era do? They organized the Jerusalem Council. The Bible says, "The apostles and elders came together to consider this matter" (Acts 15:6). What was the result? A Holy Spirit-driven decree came out of that meeting, which did not compel the Gentile converts to the burden of circumcision for matters relating to their salvation (Acts 15:22–29). Is that not what we should do today with eschatology, free will, predestination, delicate political decisions, and other topics dividing us, too? Truth is, the Holy Spirit can help us move in one direction if we trust Him and ask Him for wisdom and guidance.

## SUFFICIENCY

The Bible has sufficient arguments to survive on its own with no external pieces of evidence. It interprets itself. True, we may not understand a few things the way we do with the presence of external evidence, but that would not reduce the efficacy of its claims. For instance, historical research helps to understand the cultural settings and traditions of the nations that surrounded God's people in Bible times. History gives us more details about the mentality and practices of the Jews, Canaanites, Amalekites, Jebusites, Assyrians, Babylonians, Persians, etc. Even without this external historical research knowledge on these ancient communities, God gives us sufficient clues about their practices in Leviticus 18.

Theology cannot survive on its own. The Bible inspires authentic theology. Good theology starts and moves outside from the Bible, not from outside into the Bible.

95

We rely on biblical claims to carry out theological research. Sometimes, theologians feel a need to assume or suggest some things to fill in certain information gaps to facilitate research. But their guesswork is not always correct, and that can lead a mass of people astray. Moreover, earlier, we saw humans are full of pride. Even in the absence of sufficient evidence in support of their claims, many continue to hold to their positions because of pride.

The biggest problem with cults, for instance, is they mix truth with error, believe in extra-biblical sources of authority, reject, or devalue Christ Jesus, and compromise justification by grace alone. The consequence is that all cult adherents have a false perception of life and the future. This false perception negatively affects the way they behave.

People in a village without a trained pastor can read the Bible in their language, come to the knowledge of the truth, and keep fellowship with one another. Jesus' disciples did not go to theological schools or a seminary. All they did was observe what Jesus did. When Jesus left, they preached what they saw and did what He did or asked them to do. Before they left, they wrote what they saw and did. We continue from where they left off. Our current generations can also read about their thoughts and deeds from the Bible and do the same.

Theologians can develop their theologies to infinity; there is no limit. Our knowledge of theology is never enough. We always look for more. There is the danger. Solomon says, "In the multitude of words sin is not lacking, but he who restrains his lips is wise" (Proverbs 10:19). Sometimes, all we need is to read the Bible and accept what it says. However, some theologians come up with many explanations and interpretations that lead to confusion and error.

Keep this in mind: The Word of God has the power to accomplish what it says because God backs it. God says:

> For as the rain comes down, and the snow from Heaven, And do not return there, But water the earth, And make it bring forth and bud, That it may give seed to the sower And bread to the eater, so shall My word be that goes forth from My mouth; It shall not return to Me void, But it shall accomplish what I please, And it shall prosper in the thing for which I sent it (Isaiah 55:10–11).

Paul says, "For I am not ashamed of the gospel of Christ, for it is the power of God to salvation for everyone who believes, for the Jew first and also for the Greek" (Romans 1:16). Theology helps us to improve on our knowledge of God, but it does not have the power to move mountains. Theology always requires a foundation upon which it can flourish, and that foundation is the Bible.

> "Christian theology must affirm the sufficiency of Scripture, that it is a comprehensive source of information, instruction, and guidance. The Bible contains the whole will of God, including the information a person needs for salvation, spiritual development, and personal guidance. It contains sufficient information so that, if one were to fully obey it, he would fulfill the will of God in every detail of life, and he sins to the extent he disobeys. Although we will not attain perfect obedience in this life, it remains that the Bible contains all the information required to live a perfect Christian life."[43]

## CONSISTENCY

The Bible's message is consistent. From the fall of humanity in the Garden of Eden, we see God make a way to reunite with us. He calls Noah, Abraham, Isaac, Jacob, and our forebears, makes covenants with them, and unveils His plans for humanity. He sends prophets to tell us about what those plans are. As time passes, we see things fall in line. Jesus comes and makes a way for us to rekindle our fellowship with God. We wait for His return to reign with Him and to take us to our

---

[43] *Cheung, Theology, 31*

eternal homes. The principal focus of the Bible is Jesus the Messiah. We see this from Genesis to Revelation.

When mixed with bias, subjectivity, and prejudice, theology becomes very inconsistent. There are theologies that value some parts of the Bible more than others. For instance, some Christian organizations base their entire ministry on prosperity. They interpret every verse in the Bible to suit a message of prosperity. Other organizations idolize holiness to mean a Christian can't make a mistake, causing many to ignore depending on the Holy Spirit to take positive risks. The result of all these deviations is a religious, unbalanced Christian lifestyle. But take note of this truth: it is also possible to be consistent to some extent with a message that devalues God.

Only the Holy Spirit can guide us to embrace a balanced theology that adds value to the Bible's content. He alone can help us develop good theologies and avoid the false teachings out there. It makes sense to say a consistent theologian is one who reads his or her Bible daily, understands its content, and makes advancements based on what the Bible says. So good theology stays in line with the entirety of God's revelations in Scripture and doesn't deviate from the fundamental message of the Bible.

## PURPOSE

God wrote the Bible for all humans. As said earlier, with the Holy Spirit's help, anyone can read it with an open heart and come to the knowledge of the truth: Jesus. Through the Bible, we learn about God and His will for humankind. The Bible tells us how to put His will into practice in our lives. This purpose has not changed. It will not change until Jesus returns and puts an end to the current patterns.

Theologians sometimes develop a theology to satisfy a particular school of thought. Then you hear statements such as, "This is how we approach the situation in our school of thought," or, "We believe and see things from this angle." There is a difference between developing a theology to clarify an aspect of the Bible, say same-sex marriage or the unforgivable sin, and developing a theology to manipulate a group of people to adhere to your disputable position which the community of Christian scholars has no unanimous assurance is true. This is one danger of claiming to belong to a particular denomination, group, or system of thought. There is always a great chance your thoughts are contaminated by bias and subjective reasoning. Why? Because you naturally feel the need to defend your cycle of thoughts. Little by little, you deviate from authentic Christian positions. Because each one of these deviations, standing alone, looks insignificant, you don't realize you are on the highway to compromise. Only when you diligently look back at the bulk of ideas you generated over time do you discover most of your efforts focused more on defending your school of thought than propagating a balanced, edifying message built upon the foundation of Scripture.

We know the Bible is a diverse book; its content encourages diversity. In fact, it is illogical to expect all Christians in all places of the world to see everything the same way. People have traditions and customs that do not contradict the Scriptures. In most Islamic traditions, people eat together with their hands from the same plate and drink from the same cup. That's normal there. So, Christians in an Islamic country would enjoy drinking from the same cup when taking communion. Westerners would each have their own glass and piece of bread. They are not used to eating or drinking from the same items. But both traditions glorify God in their diversity. A common doctrine binds these Muslim converts and the Western ones together. They won't have any problem moving along or working together for the kingdom's sake.

Compare that with the Jehovah's Witness theology about Jesus. They demote Him to a prophet and refuse any theology about Him being God. They go as far as rewriting the Bible, subtracting from it, and adding to it so it matches their claims. When we study their

JOHN MWAFISE WOLOKO

methods, way of action, theology, and approach to evangelism, we discover a cult that cannot lead any of its followers to the true light, Jesus. But they work tirelessly, knock on doors, preach daily, and print all sorts of magazines and articles. Unfortunately, most of what they propagate centers around defending their school of thought, not revealing Jesus to the unsaved. Far worse, their theologies don't start from the Bible to the outside, rather, from the outside into the Bible. They have to rewrite the Bible for their message to conform to their ideas. Genuine Christians cannot move along with them because they disagree on the fundamental doctrine.

Think of it: had the disciples not organized the Jerusalem Council, what would have happened? Obviously, they would have allowed two self-seeking groups of Christians with contradicting beliefs and practices to claim the truth and put others in confusion. That would have compromised the propagation of the gospel in their times. That is exactly what the Arminians, Calvinists, Preterists, etc., have failed to do today. Hence, dozens of groups, all claiming to be authentic Christians, with contradicting foundational presuppositions, fight to exist. Is Jesus divided? Does diversity compromise unity? You answer the questions for yourself.

## TABLE OF DIFFERENCES

| The Bible | Theology |
|---|---|
| Contains God's Word and will to humanity | The method we use to interpret what God reveals in the Bible and universe by presenting pieces of evidence in an organized manner. |
| Inspired by the Holy Spirit | Not always inspired by the Holy Spirit. Sometimes, bias, subjectivity, and prejudice find their way into it. |
| Always true and authentic | Not everything is true. Some thoughts are human opinions, assumptions, and suggestions. Only true when the Holy Spirit inspires it and biblical revelations motivate it. |

| | |
|---|---|
| Sufficient: A believer can survive only with it. He or she can't see the light without it. | Cannot survive on its own. Never enough. Theologians can develop it to infinity. At some point, you get tired of it. |
| Consistent and trustworthy | Sometimes lacks logical congruency, trustworthiness, and truthfulness. It confuses and complicates some topics with difficult terms. |
| Interprets itself sufficiently with the help of the Holy Spirit | Sometimes, the theologians don't allow the Word of God to interpret itself. They add to or subtract from God's Word. |
| Written and preserved for everyone in the world | The different schools of thought will never agree. Scholars will adhere only to what they accept, |

except they humble themselves and organize something like the Jerusalem Conference.

| | |
|---|---|
| As he or she reads its content, the Holy Spirit guides the believer to discern truth and apply it in life. | The believer needs a teacher. The teacher is only correct if the Holy Spirit inspires him or her. |
| Some things in it are difficult to understand, but through meditation, the Holy Spirit clarifies. | Theologians complicate many difficult Bible passages with their opinions, biases, and subjective approaches. |
| An unbeliever needs its content to know Jesus, be saved, and practice a holy lifestyle. | Helps to understand some details about God and God's doctrines when inspired by the Holy Spirit. But an unbeliever can't find salvation in it. |

| | |
|---|---|
| Encourages unity, love, and peace among believers. | Can instigate disunity, hatred, arguments, quarrels, and intellectual pride when mishandled. |

Chapter Six

# HOW TO USE
# THE BIBLE AND THEOLOGY

## UNDERSTAND THEIR ROLES

B efore we even think of any use of the Bible and theology, we must understand their roles. Yes, we must know the place each one of them occupies in the fields of wisdom and knowledge acquisition. We looked at the similarities and differences between the Bible and theology. We discovered the Bible can survive on its own without theology. The Bible inspires every good theology we have out there. Theology doesn't inspire the Bible, but the Bible inspires every good theology. The Bible is greater than theology in all aspects. We limit the role of theology to bringing additional clarification to some areas of the Bible we may have difficulties in understanding. Theology does so by providing additional pieces of evidence from within or outside the Bible.

Therefore, we shouldn't compare theology to the Bible. We can't put them on the same scale, but we must remember theology plays a significant role in our interpretation and understanding of the Bible. Each time we engage in theological activity, we must keep in mind we only want to have a clearer understanding of the Scriptures. The primary objective is either to build ourselves up in the faith or win souls into God's kingdom.

Therefore, no theological explanation can take the place of biblical revelations. It is our engagement in meditating on these biblical revelations that helps us develop theologies that add value to those revelations. If the Holy Spirit guides us, we learn to put bias, subjectivity, and prejudice aside, and we develop excellent theologies that support the Scriptures all the time. This leads to the second wise use of both.

## PREACH GOD'S WORD, TEACH THEOLOGY

Yes, this may sound funny, but we've got to preach God's Word in the Bible and teach theology. Some would argue this makes little sense. Let's see why it makes so much more sense than you can imagine.

One reason is that many people haven't learned to separate the Bible's message from the supporting evidence coming from the field of theology. That is why many go so far as to say we won't survive without theology. In the days of Moses, all they did was read the Law and talk about it. In fact, no other person had the Law at home. They came to one spot to listen to God's message. Jesus' disciples and early Christians didn't go to theological schools, as we said earlier, but many of us in this generation have yet to match their level of impact. All the disciples of Jesus did was talk about what they saw Jesus doing. The writer of Hebrews says, "...the word of God is living and powerful..." (Hebrews 4:14). Paul says he is "...not ashamed of the gospel of Christ, for it is the power of God to salvation for everyone who believes..." (Romans 1:16).

Power and salvation are not in theology, rather in God's Word. Many theologians are ashamed of the gospel but not of their theology. They deny Jesus is the Messiah and refuse to talk about Him in public for fear of persecution, but they have and represent a theology about the Bible and Jesus which is of no use. We make it our mission to preach the Word of God, because in it is the power that saves those who hear and believe. Our primary mission is not to engage in unending theological explanations; rather, it is to read, listen to, and preach God's Word.

Most theological explanations add to the existing confusion. We don't need to understand everything about Jesus for Him to save us. All we need is sufficient knowledge about Him found in the Bible. God's power in that knowledge does the rest of the saving work. John says, "And there are also many other things that Jesus did, which if they were written one by one, I suppose that even the world itself could not contain the books that would be written" (John 21:25). What we know about Him in the Bible is enough.

We don't need to know everything about a job to do it. A pilot doesn't need to understand every bit of detail about an aircraft to fly it. In fact, plane manufacturers constantly update their software to perform better. The government doesn't recruit the classroom teacher because he or she knows everything about the subject. The mechanic doesn't know everything about your car. We will never reach complete knowledge of any subject. There is always room to increase in knowledge. Who is the Christian who accepts Jesus because he or she knows everything about Him?

So, a preacher proclaims God's message for the moment to the audience. Whenever a preacher does his job, in reality, the Holy Spirit works through the person. So, the audience keeps quiet and listens to God's message through the preacher. The Holy Spirit is God. There's no room for argument with Him. We are not His advisers either.

We teach theology because we want to add to our existing understanding of what the Bible already says, not because of any additional revelations. Theology comes with discoveries that bring more light to the

Scriptures—nothing more, nothing less. But how do we know that theology brings added value? We teach it or expose it out there because we want to give everyone the chance to evaluate it, critique it, and bring further arguments to it. Who has enough intellectual capacity to critique the Word of God? Yet, we don't expect a theologian to say Jesus is not God, even though that contradicts the Bible, then go and preach it from the pulpit. No way! And we don't want another theologian to say the Dead Sea Scrolls add to the authenticity of the Bible without verifying whether those claims are true.

Therefore, we preach what is authentic, but we teach what needs authentication to allow an evaluation through reason. Teaching is an interactive activity. If we discover a theology we think can help, what do we do? The natural reaction is to bring it out there for scrutiny. The community of true believers examines it to discover the value the theology brings to the Bible before they adopt it as a true doctrine. If your theology is weak, inconsistent or inaccurate, you must be sincere and back down.

Is that what we see today? No! The Arminians come from an angle—Calvinists from a contrary one. Like two negative magnetic poles repelling each other, they never agree. Yet, each group continues to develop and preach their theology, even though they know their other brothers and sisters won't agree with them. The result is intellectual pride and divisions. Who should we believe? Are your theological explanations greater than what the Bible says? Who cares about the eloquence of your beautiful speeches? As long as your theology doesn't unite Christians who hold to the core doctrines, something is wrong somewhere. Yes, your theology may contribute to research and improve our knowledge on certain topics, but it shows limitations you must accept. We can take the good from it and dump the rest. You have to stop preaching it in the pulpits.

The Bible clearly says we can agree and move in one direction. In fact, the Bible takes another approach to gaining knowledge, understanding, and interpreting the Scriptures. See what it says:

> ...fulfill my joy by being like-minded, having the same love, being of one accord, of one mind. Let nothing be done through selfish ambition or conceit, but in lowliness of mind let each esteem others better than himself. Let each of you look out not only for his own interests, but also for the interests of others (Philippians 2:2–4).

Is this what Catholics are doing with their Presbyterian and Reformed brethren? Can we boldly say Arminians and Calvinists are in harmony with these verses? Who then should we believe: your lengthy theologies or what the Bible says? If your position is not in harmony with what the Bible says, who is to blame?

It is sad some spiritual leaders stand in the pulpits and preach theology when theology is only useful in differentiating, recognizing, and discovering what is of divine origin and what is not. Although we can mention theological teachings in preaching, the objective is only to confirm God's Word. We illustrate how the theology accomplishes that without diverting the attention of the audience from the Word of God. Yet, many preachers bring theology to their pulpits because they want to promote their position or school of thought. This habit nourishes and produces most of the confusion in the Body of Christ. This ultimately gives rise to intellectual pride, a prevailing characteristic in numerous contemporary churches that should inspire us to adopt the same attitude as the Berean Christians in Paul's time (Acts 17:10-11).

## KNOW YOUR CALLING AND AREA OF

## SPECIALIZATION

If our objective for studying theology is not to know more of God, His revelations in the Bible, and obey His will, we study in vain and build on sinking sand. The Bible tells us, "Let all things be done decently and in order" (1 Corinthians 14:40). If God has a plan for our lives, we can't live our Christian life as though there is none. We make it our mission to discover His short- and long-term projects for our lives and strive to carry them out. Some insights on the direction in which God wants to lead us help us to determine the type of extra-biblical knowledge we want to gain.

Let's assume the Holy Spirit urges you to go down to the streets and talk to unbelievers about Jesus. You can't ignore that those people you talk to come from different theological backgrounds. Some are atheists; others are occult members; many belong to Christian cults and pagan religions, and a good number don't want to hear anything about God.

So, how do you prepare yourself to go down to the street and talk to people? You study your Bible and understand its content. You know the core message everyone must hear from your mouth: Jesus died for their sins, rose again from the dead, and will return soon. Anyone can receive Jesus and escape everlasting punishment caused by sin, and this salvation is a gift from God, free for all.

A few will respond to this core message from the Bible, probably because other preachers sowed seeds in their lives, and the Holy Spirit convicts their hearts to give up their selfishness and accept Jesus once and for all at that moment. However, the majority will question your beliefs based on the knowledge they gained in their own theological upbringings. You must confront the ideas of the latter if you want God to use you to win them into His kingdom.

Hence, you strengthen your understanding of the Bible with theological explanations. You've got to know what the various groups of people who confront you believe in. So, you study pre-suppositional apologetics, understand the foundational doctrines of the various worldviews out there, how to refute them, and you present the gospel to them. Because there are so many worldviews out there, you want to specialize in one or a few at a time to be effective. Maybe organize conferences, debates, workshops, or create an internet platform to confront as many people you can reach as possible.

As a person who spends most of his or her ministry on the streets, it would be inefficient to study for a pastoral degree. Although most scholars agree that a pastor should be a wonderful teacher of the Word as well, the pastor's primary role is to take care of a group of people God put under his responsibility. So, a pastor would choose theological courses that help to build and strengthen the church. One who confronts Islam or evolution would study those subjects in significant detail.

We make the best use of theology when we have some knowledge of the area in which God wants us to work. Then, we study theological courses that help us be efficient in that area. We study theology because we want to add essential knowledge to the Scriptures, not because the Scriptures don't say enough about themselves.

Our objective for engaging in theological activity is to add to our veracity, conviction, and efficiency in answering God's call in that area and better serve one another. Theological exercise does not give room for Christians to grow in pride. Even when we deal with unbelievers, the Bible tells us to "…always be ready to give a defense to everyone who asks you a reason for the hope that is in you, with meekness and fear" (1 Peter 3:15–16). Notice we engage in that activity with meekness and fear, not pride and arrogance.

## FOCUS ON THE AGENDA

Remember, we've got the Bible—and it is sufficient. If we would study nothing else but the Bible, we would still survive. Here comes the question: Why, then, do we engage in theological activity? This is a serious question. Solomon makes a point we must all consider in our acquisition of knowledge: "Of making many books there is no end, and much study is wearisome to the flesh" (Ecclesiastes 12:12). In the last section, we talked about knowing our calling, but it is equally important to have an agenda. The agenda is like a vision that guides your mission or calling. Let me show this with an example:

Let's assume God calls you to pastor a church and plant other churches in a region. You obey the call and plant the first church. This church grows big. The Holy Spirit urges you to plant the second. So, you dispatch some members of your church to start another branch in another location of the region under your guidance. This one grows, too. You go in for the third in another location of the same region.

As you plant the fourth church in that region, you discover members of your church get into momentary arguments with members of another denomination that also plants churches. In your research, you discover this other denomination has different traditions and approaches to evangelism, although all your core doctrines are the same.

What do you do? You plunge into a mission to expose what you believe are mistakes in the theology of the other denomination. You organize debates to argue with members of the other denomination. With time, members of both denominations switch sides. Others leave both organizations completely because of the confusion your debates create. Your engagements later transform into hatred. Members of the two movements can't marry among each other. Many years have passed since you last planted another church. A good number of your loyal members left your church. Those who stayed have no vision save momentary evangelism. You still compete with the other denominations in that region.

What would have been the best way to react in this situation? The moment you discovered clashes between believers of your movement and those of the other, you should have realized there is not much to evangelize in that region. It is as simple as that. That was the time to break camp and move inter-regionally and internationally.

God gave us an agenda to win souls and build them up in His ways as long as we are still in this world. This is the general agenda by which every Christian individual and organization works; the agenda determines the goals. This agenda is true for both your organization and the others you fight against. Aside from this general agenda, every individual Holy-Spirit-filled Christian organization has a specific agenda. Your specific agenda was to plant churches. That was probably the agenda of the other denomination, too. You both fell out of this agenda the moment you started confronting each other in unnecessary debates on traditions and customs.

Think about it. You both have minor differences in your theologies, but the core doctrines remain intact. There is no hindrance to the gospel. This is a simple diversity, which has nothing to do with the efficacy of each organization winning souls and planting churches. The proof is that both movements planted many churches. Instead of exploring outside the region, you wasted your resources in unnecessary confrontations. Diversity will always exist in the Body of Christ, and genuine diversity does not compromise unity. Theological contradictions, not diversity, are the threat to unity. You wasted your time fighting diversity, a battle you can never win. You misunderstood God's general agenda for His church and for you as an individual Christian movement. Your members left for another organization because God no longer met their needs through yours. You could have joined forces with the other movement to win the remaining unbelievers in the region you compete for and develop strategies to reach the outside world. Instead, you wasted your time in futilities and planted churches no further. Paul describes your behavior as follows; "...strive about words to no profit, to the ruin of the hearers" (2 Timothy 2:14).

Chapter Seven

# SCRIPTURE INTERPRETATION

After gaining much valuable information in previous chapters, I think it's a good time to fold everything up with Scripture interpretation. What's the proper way to unfold God's message in Bible passages? Are there rules to follow when interpreting the Scriptures? Who defines those rules? How can we be sure our interpretation is correct? Before answering these questions, remember that we said theology's major role is to bring additional pieces of evidence to support biblical revelations. Theological insights can never be equal to the written Word, Yet, when used correctly, a theology inspires and broadens our understanding of God's will.

So, the objective of any Holy Spirit-filled child of God is to know and do God's will at each point in time. We want to generate the best Bible-centered thoughts every time we read Bible passages. Given the close connection between the Bible and its inspired theologies, the reader finds value in knowing the principles of Scripture interpretation. He or she learns to spot common errors and logical fallacies and engages in "casting down arguments and every high thing that exalts itself against the knowledge of God, bringing every thought into captivity to the obedience of Christ" (2 Corinthians 10:5).

## THE SUPREME GUIDE

At the core of any correct interpretation of the Scriptures is the One who inspired them—God. The Bible declares, "All Scripture is given by inspiration of God..." (2 Timothy 3:16). In Chapter One, we dove deep into the reasons God gave us the Bible: "for doctrine, reproof, correction, and instruction in righteousness." We do God's will as a result. We can verify we're on the right path through the fruits He guides us to bear for Him. Given God is the inspirer of Scriptures for these purposes, there's no way we can get anything right about understanding or using His inspired Word if He doesn't guide us. For this reason, He gave us the Holy Spirit to "teach us all things, remind us of what we learned from the Bible and guide us into all truth" (John 14:25, 16:13–15).

Before you open your Bible, read what's written in it, meditate or apply any reasoning, you must have committed your entire body, mind, soul, and spirit to the Holy Spirit for guidance. This is the first step. If you neglect Him, you beat around the bush. Because many of us put the Holy Spirit aside or refuse to give Him His proper place, the thoughts we generate don't converge.

## UNITY

The Holy Spirit can't lie. God doesn't contradict Himself. He means what He says. Scripture says we should "...be like-minded, having the same love, being of one accord, of one mind" (Philippians 2:2). Don't ask if this is possible. Why would God inspire such things if they aren't possible? With Him, all things are possible. To be of one mind is not just a desired ideal in God's eyes. That's how He expects us to relate to one another. There's plenty of evidence in Scripture to support His position. The early believers understood the power behind unity in faith. "Now the multitude of those who believed were of one heart and one soul...." "And through the hands of the apostles many signs and wonders were done among the people. And they were all with one accord in Solomon's Porch" (Acts 4:32—5:12).

There was no Catholic, Presbyterian, Baptist, Methodist, Evangelical, Apostolic, Protestant, Calvinist, Arminian, Preterist, etc. I know what just popped up in your mind. Christians of those days were not plenty. They hadn't faced the challenges of a much bigger Christian community like there is today. Yet, not too far from those Pentecostal days, in the middle of an established Christian church, Paul warned the Ephesians to:

> ...walk worthy of the calling with which you were called, with all lowliness and gentleness, with longsuffering, bearing with one another in love, endeavoring to keep the unity of the Spirit in the bond of peace. There is one body and one Spirit, just as you were called in one hope of your calling; one Lord, one faith, one baptism; one God and Father of all, who is above all, and through all, and in you all (Ephesians 4:1–6).

Paul was definitely saddened by what he noticed—notably, divisions among fellow believers in Christ.

Speaking to the Corinthian church, he said, "For you are still carnal. For where there are envy, strife, and divisions among you, are you not carnal and behaving like mere men? For when one says, 'I am of Paul,' and another, 'I am of Apollos,' are you not carnal?" (1 Corinthians 3-4). He spoke concerning their divisions, "Now I say this, that each of you says, 'I am of Paul,' or 'I am of Apollos,' or 'I am of Cephas,' or 'I am of Christ.' Is Christ divided? Was Paul crucified for you? Or were you baptized in the name of Paul?" (1 Corinthians 1:12–13). Today, some of you say, "I am of John Calvin," and others, "I am of Jacobus

Arminius." "I am Reformed, Catholic, Methodist." Is Christ divided? Is His church divided? Were you baptized in the name of Calvin or Arminius?

How ridiculous we have become! To the extent that our leaders even use the vacuous phrase, "Let's agree to disagree." We can't see how low we've fallen from God's standard. When dealing with scriptural interpretation, either we agree or disagree. He who stands between the two camps is Truth. God can't tell a believer one thing about a Scripture and then tell another believer something contradictory about the same Scripture so that they fight each other about who is correct. No, that's not God. If we want to know His position, all we have to do is seek His face, and He promises to tell us if we approach Him sincerely (James 1:5).

The statements above can confuse the reader. But there's no room for too much thinking on our part in this issue. The Body of Christ is a single movement with standard rules that apply to all, regardless of your location on the globe, your race, and even your cultural settings. God's principles of unity transcend any type of barrier. He doesn't ask us to be Catholics, Calvinists, Reformers, Preterists, etc. We created those movements with our overlearning. It's a fact that these unnecessary segregations have helped to compromise our unity in the faith.

The reader should distinguish two things. The first is the Logos Word of God—everything the Holy Spirit inspired and wrote through His servants in the Bible. In recording any verse or passage of Scripture, He had one meaning and interpretation for it in mind. That meaning may or may not apply to our current setting (we will elaborate on this later). But there's always something to learn from any Bible passage. This leads to the second thing the reader must distinguish—the rhema Word of God, which are insights we generate by reading Scriptures to help us navigate through the issues of life. The Logos serve as roots or a foundation. The rhemas are the branches, fruits, or building. If you get the Logos right, the rhemas you generate will bear many fruits; if the Logos is wrong, you find limitations in your Christian walk.

What do we mean? There's no problem calling yourself Catholic, Arminian, Methodist, or Seventh Days Adventist if you all have the same interpretation of the Logos and generate rhemas that edify one another. In fact, call yourself what you want; that's part of diversity. Remember, we said diversity stems from our cultural, environmental and racial settings in this physical world. Christians who sing and dance with various instruments shouldn't have any problem moving along with those who sing only hymns and clap hands. The Holy Spirit testifies they are all children of God with no doubt in mind. True diversity does not inspire contradictions. Instead, it enables God to use us effectively in our context. His gift of diversity makes Christians less boring.

However, there's a problem if you call yourself Catholic, Protestant, Evangelical, Methodist, or Reformed and you don't agree with each other on what the Logos says. Sad to say, here is where most of us find ourselves. These movements have fundamental differences in their foundational beliefs. God isn't the author of this confusion. His standard is agreement. We must not turn around it. Calling ourselves these names and not agreeing on the Logos is lowering His standard. It's as simple as that. No, the Holy Spirit can't inspire contradictions. Let's humble ourselves and seek His face for truth. He knows how to lead us in the same direction.

## COMMONSENSE IN THE LOGOS

There's no need to complicate matters with exaggerated study and definition of terms. It only confuses people the more and makes it harder for those outside the faith to discover and embrace truth. Let's keep things simple. The terms "Logos," "Scripture," "Word of God," "Word of Life," "God's Word," etc., all point to everything the Holy Spirit inspired His servants to write and compile in the Bible. But let's not approach the Logos as though we were people without a reasoning faculty. Some parts of the Logos are statements God made. Others are not God's Words, rather things ordinary believers and unbelievers said. But all sections of the Logos are things the Holy Spirit inspired His servants to write.

God told Abraham, "Get out of your country, from your family and from your father's house, to a land that I will show you" (Genesis 12:1). He told Joshua, "...arise, go over this Jordan, you and all this people, to a land which I am giving to them—the children of Israel" (Joshua 1:2). Ananias heard God say in a vision, "Arise and go to the street called Straight and inquire at the house of Judas for one called Saul of Tarsus..." (Acts 9:11). Neither God nor the Holy Spirit inspired Tobias the Ammonite to say of Nehemiah's project, "Whatever they build, if even a fox goes up on it, he will break down their stone wall" (Nehemiah 4:3). But the Holy Spirit inspired Nehemiah to record Tobias' words for our learning. He guided the apostles in the same manner to write the things in the gospels, the Book of Acts, and the letters to the church.

Furthermore, the Bible says, "And Jacob set a pillar on her grave, which is the pillar of Rachel's grave to this day" (Genesis 35:20). "And the king of Ai he hanged on a tree until evening. And as soon as the sun was down, Joshua commanded that they should take his corpse down from the tree, cast it at the entrance of the gate of the city, and raise over it a great heap of stones that remains to this day" (Joshua 8:29). The Bible describes a part of the Jewish temple, "The poles extended so that the ends of the poles could be seen from the holy place, in front of the inner sanctuary; but they could not be seen from outside. And they are there to this day" (1 Kings 8:8).

Would you go around looking for the pillar of Rachel's grave today? If you don't find it, does that make the statement or Bible false? Or we must determine the exact location of Joshua's heap of stones to prove the Bible, right? If those poles in Solomon's temple aren't there to this day, he who wrote that part of the Bible is a liar. Aren't such conclusions ridiculous?

What does common sense tell you about such statements? Even if we can occasionally use archaeology to prove them, to arrive at such conclusions is void of common logic. A pile of stones made four thousand years ago must have turned into dust and sand. Rachel's grave is probably underneath a city building. The context has changed; the world has moved on. There was a time when we could verify those ancient signs, boundaries, and landmarks. A time comes when they deteriorate if there's no policy in place to protect them. Those the Holy Spirit used recorded those statements when those things were still physically verifiable.

Likewise, no one in his or her right senses can read the Bible and say, "I don't see God the Father, Son, and Holy Spirit." This mystery troubles many a theologian or worldly intellectual. Call it what you want—trinity,

God is One, whatever. The truth is that you can't play around with these three. The more you meditate on the Logos, the more you discover they are distinct but the same. The Holy Spirit does what the Father and Son do. The Father and the Son are One. Yet, they are distinct. No, I can't explain it, but there's no way you can read the Bible and claim not to see them. We may lack the eloquence to explain the mystery, but commonsense tells us it is there. We can see their effects in our Christian walk.

## COMMONSENSE IN THE RHEMA

Get this right: the rhema Word of God comes from the Logos. The Logos produce many rhemas. There is no limit to the number of rhemas a single verse in the Bible can generate. Just like the Bible and the theologies it inspires are distinct, so are rhemas and the Logos different. One can't take the place of the other. The Logos is the Bible's content. The insights the Holy Spirit guides us to generate from this written Word are rhemas.

Commonsense tells us to be careful with rhemas. They may be false—not inspired by the Holy Spirit. For instance, Herod learned Christ will be born in Bethlehem in the Land of Judea. That's what the Logos says. So, he told the Wise Men from the East, "Go search carefully for the young Child, and when you have found Him, bring back words to me, that I may come and worship Him also" (Mathew 2:8). Did he really want to worship Jesus? No, he was only looking for a way to kill him. False prophets misuse rhemas to deceive their followers to enrich themselves. All false prophets hide their evil in their popularity, eloquence of speech, and outstanding motivational messages. This makes it hard for untrained and immature Christians to discover their tricks.

You can't and shouldn't try to change a Logos (Matthew 5:18). The Logos is the standard, the foundation. You build on that foundation by using rhemas, which depend on your calling, situation, and context. You will generate or come across millions of them in life but only a few are beneficial to your life and calling. Many rhemas don't apply to your context or case. Each stage of your life has its own beneficial rhemas. Most of the time, you generate the rhemas you need in life from the Logos yourself. That's why you must develop a personal relationship with God and read your Bible daily. Then the Holy Spirit can inspire you to generate unique, useful, and effective rhemas to accomplish your mission and bring glory to God.

On a few occasions, God may use another person or situation in life to guide you. Most of the time, however, you've got to learn to listen to your inner man. So never develop the habit of relying on someone else for rhemas. It doesn't work like that. God expects you to read and meditate on the Logos so you can produce the rhemas you need to do the works He has for you. That's how it works. Whenever God sees you need help, He knows how to guide your steps to someone who can help you.

Can you see why many get into troubles? They don't read the Logos. They have their favorite pastor or prophet who they claim prays for them and gives them precise prophesies. What a slow way to kill the gifts and skills God gave them. No, you don't need to study theology to know these things. It's simple common sense. Why would someone ask you to give a tithe or sell your car or house for a miraculous prayer, and you accept? Only because of your ignorance! The Logos says, "Let us therefore come boldly to the throne of grace, that we may obtain mercy and find grace to help in time of need" (Hebrews 4:16). Approach God. He will guide your steps to find solutions to your problems.

Therefore, when we interpret the Bible, we learn to distinguish between the Logos and the rhemas the Logos generates. But it doesn't end there. We trust God to make sure there is a clear link between the Logos and its inspired rhemas. Finally, we ask the Holy Spirit to show us which rhemas can help us and how to apply them in our individual situations.

## THE HUMAN BEING

The human being has a natural tendency to do things contrary to God's will. Reluctance and rebellion have a grip on us. Even when we come to Christ, we still struggle with the effects of the sting of death from the Garden of Eden. The only way to get things right all the time is a total dependence on the Holy Spirit. Yet, show me one person who claims to depend on the Holy Spirit every single time, and I will show you a million playing religiosity. When interpreting the Scriptures, we must keep in mind that we learn every day. Not all of us are on the same spiritual level. For these reasons, training is helpful in filling some gaps of knowledge and boosting our trust in God.

We make errors because we introduce bias, prejudice, and subjectivity into the Logos. It happens based on the type of philosophical knowledge we gained before coming across Scripture. Those who aren't born again do this all the time. The born again who doesn't rely on the Holy Spirit does it every time he or she sets Him aside. Ignorance and lack of knowledge of Bible times affect the way we interpret the Scriptures. Human communication evolves with time. Many words have multiple meanings. Despite the flexibility of our languages, we still find difficulties explaining the things of God in their contexts. When interpreting the Scriptures, we must consider the context in which the writer wrote before determining how it applies to us today. Failure to do this puts us off track.

## DIFFICULTIES IN SCRIPTURE

The Bible's message is simple, but it is not straightforward. One must read through Genesis to Revelation to grasp the full meaning of what Jesus accomplished on the Cross of Calvary and its implications for our lives as Christians today. Stitching Scriptures together from the Old to the New Testament to come up with that coherent Bible message is an art. To succeed in this endeavor, one needs a fair level of concentration and the Holy Spirit's leadership. The Bible our forebears compiled with the help of the Holy Spirit presents some challenges. We must consider these challenges if we want to make sense of what God wants to communicate to us.

Looking into history, there's no way we can have the original texts of Scripture. Back then, when God spoke to Moses, there were no printing machines and books as we have today, yet they did everything in their capacity to preserve the message. What we find today are hand copies of copies of the original texts.

> "Any type of copying is bound to introduce errors of spelling, repetition, omission, and others; the problem is compounded when this process of hand-copying is repeated for

hundreds or thousands of years without the help of modern writing aids. In fact, many of the ancient nonbiblical books have altered so much in this process that sometimes up to 90% of the extant text of a book is corrupted. However, those men who copied the books of the Bible knew they were not handling an ordinary book, so they took exceptional care during hand-copying. As a result, the number of errors that have crept into the biblical manuscripts is minimal compared to other ancient manuscripts."[44]

"Another difficulty of the original text is the language. The ancient Hebrews did not write like the modern man. Their language had only capital letters. Further, they wrote words without vowels and, to compound the problem, these words were not separated from each other. This process resulted in some errors of translation in the King James Version that most people use in English. Some of these errors have crept into other languages. However, the tens of thousands of ancient biblical manuscripts available today have helped Bible scholars to restore the original text with great certainty."[45]

[44] *Dr. Saneesh And Dr. Philip, Bible Difficulties, 1–3*
[45] *Dr. Saneesh And Dr. Philip, Bible Difficulties, 2–6*

Given the complexity of the original language of Scripture, we have had difficulties translating the Bible into other languages over the years, as noted by Dr. Johnson C. Philip and Dr. Saneesh Cherian:

> "The difficulty increases manyfold when idiomatic expressions from an extinct language, representing the speech pattern of an ancient society, has to be translated into the present-day speech... Sometimes, a Hebrew or Greek word can be translated by many different words of another language, none of which might be adequate for a satisfactory translation...The original autographs of the Bible were verbally inspired by God, and therefore, they are inerrant and infallible, but the same is not true of translations. The paraphrases are removed further from the original text. Even the most faithful translation of the Bible contains some paraphrases, biases of the translators, wrong equivalents, and also archaisms. Archaic words are those which have lost or changed their original meaning so that they no longer mean what the translator intended them to mean."[46]

The Bible deals with history, geography, politics, ethics, psychology, human relationships, ancient and future mysteries, etc. In recording those statements, the Holy

[46] *Dr. Saneesh And Dr. Philip, Bible Difficulties, 6*

Spirit-inspired writers had definite and clear-cut meanings they wanted to communicate to us. This is true because God does not relate to us with ambiguities. His intention has never been to leave us in the dark. The difficulty we have today is to understand everything the way the writer meant it. Here, we must admit we have some limitations. What do humans do with these limitations?

> "The human mind tries to solve the problem by substituting a possible interpretation for the intended meaning. Obviously, all interpretations will have a human prejudice in them and therefore the number of such interpretations might increase. Some of these interpretations might violently contradict the ideas cherished by others, and this might make a lot of people upset about the Bible. But the problem here is not with the Bible but with the differing viewpoints of the people who are trying to bring out the possible meaning or implication of the biblical text under consideration."[47]

Therefore, we engage in the exercise of Scripture interpretation with incomplete knowledge of the customs, history, geography, and the society of Bible times. Besides these, we are sometimes ignorant of the

---

[47] *Dr. Saneesh And Dr. Philip, Bible Difficulties, 9*

conditions under which the writer wrote the book, passage, or Bible verse and the reason for certain instructions. So, we have finite human beings whose approaches may harbor logical fallacies, trying to make meaning of an infinite God.

## GENERAL COMMONSENSE

What now? Is the Bible corrupt and unable to guide us today? Do all these things discussed above prove the Bible is untrue? Oh no! These are facts we must admit when approaching the Bible. We can't claim they are not there or try to turn around them, as some Bible students do. This is an amazing fact about the God of the Bible—He knows Satan has had a grip on us ever since we fell out of love with Him in the Garden of Eden. You see, the Bible doesn't claim to come down from Heaven as Muslims claim the Quran does. God used imperfect humans to write, compile, and transmit His perfect Word from one generation to the other. It's obvious He would encounter some challenges originating from our imperfect state. Of course, "…our understanding of the Bible is not complete yet, and therefore, many problems remain to be solved."[48] But our "…experience with the disappearance of some problems shows that a few unsolved problems do not prove the Bible to be wrong. And this, of course, does not prevent us from gaining an understanding of the

[48] *Dr. Saneesh And Dr. Philip, Bible Difficulties, 9*

written Word that suffices for living an abundant Christian life."[49] Our inability to answer some of these questions at the moment doesn't mean there are no solutions. "Of course, many jump into wrong kinds of conclusions occasionally, but most of the time, people have the common sense to look objectively at the issues and conclude that inability to solve does not imply that it is impossible to solve the problem. Instead, it is better to wait for more information."[50]

When we compare the excellencies of the Bible, what we gain from what we know about it and what it inspires us to accomplish, all those difficulties become insignificant. Why is this true? Because superficial readers waste their time giving more weight to these alleged insignificant difficulties compared with serious students who accomplish wonders with the sufficient knowledge they gain from Scripture. Remember, the pilot need not know every detail about the engineering of a plane to fly it. God deals with us despite our limitations.

This is another fact—those who critique the Bible have more problems in the worldviews they represent than Christians have with the Bible, but they approach the Bible as though they have attained complete knowledge in their systems of belief.

---

[49] *Dr. Saneesh And Dr. Philip, Bible Difficulties, 9*
[50] *Dr. Saneesh And Dr. Philip, Bible Difficulties, 10*

We shouldn't forget the Bible's revelations are a serious target to propagandists. Day and night, all they do is try to destroy the message of the Bible to create artificial problems—which don't originate in Scripture—to confuse the imprudent minds. We sincere Christian inquirers know where we may have difficulties in understanding some things in Scripture. We talk openly about these things, write books, and expose them out there. We trust God to give us reliable answers as we engage in genuine research. Moreover, this doesn't mean all the troubles will disappear. A problem-free system is not of this age, but of the one to come. Rather, we have gained sufficient knowledge about God to this point, although there's much more to grasp. This sufficient knowledge we gained from Scripture far exceeds those minor discrepancies. The Holy Spirit fills what seem to be gaps of knowledge with a supernatural understanding of the Father's will. Aren't we constantly experiencing God's wonders and celebrating victories?

## HOW TO DO IT CORRECTLY

### *Invite The Holy Spirit To Guide You*

Remember, the Holy Spirit's mission is to guide us to all truths. Without Him, we cannot do or know anything that brings glory to God. Already from this first step, the reader sees why many interpretations of the same texts contradict each other. We neglect Him.

God doesn't inspire divisions. Diversity in Christ does not inspire contradictions in the Logos. The Father's principles of unity stand strong and tall. He expects us all to move in the same direction, although we serve Him in diverse ways. God can't inspire interpretations that bring conflicts among us. He "is not the author of confusion but of peace..." (1 Corinthians 14:33).

We must agree on what the writers meant and the conditions under which they wrote. If we can't agree on something, let's set that aside, stick with what we agree upon, and continue to do research on what we don't agree on. No one should think his or her individual interpretation is correct amid disagreements. Only intellectual pride leads us to adopt that position. But when dealing with the rhema Word of God, it all depends on our contexts and situation. We shouldn't compare rhemas. God shows them to His children as He wills. That depends on the type of relationship and mission He has with them. One verse can generate different rhemas for many people under diverse conditions and in unique contexts.

## The Primary Meaning Of A Scripture Is What It Says

Don't add or remove from Scripture. Many of us stumble on this point. A verse or section of Scripture makes a point clear, but we navigate around it in search of additional explanations for it. This happens a lot with topics such as marriage and divorce, women occupying church leadership positions, tithing, salvation, predestination, works, etc. At this stage, it is clear there's a lot more we can agree on in the Logos than we can disagree on. Not that we focus only on what we agree on. Rather, we cherish everything we agree on but join hands together to do research on what we don't agree on with the Holy Spirit's help to avoid walking each his own way. God wants us to continue in unity.

In Acts 14:8–10, a cripple heard Paul preaching. The Bible says, "Paul, observing him intently and seeing that he had faith to be healed, said with a loud voice, 'Stand up straight on your feet!' And he leaped and walked." This verse means just what it says. That is the Logos. No one should take from it or add any other meaning to it. But there are no limits to what this little section of Scripture inspires in our Christian walk. Some see weak faith in the cripple. Others explore evangelism tactics from the same passage. Another sees a means to healing. The same Scriptures can inspire humanitarian works. It all depends on the situation and context, but we must not fail to distinguish between the Logos as it is written in its context and the rhemas it inspires. Most of the interpretation problems we have are because we read the Logos and bring our individual rhemas into it. This is contradictory to the relationship between Logos and rhemas; the former give rise to the latter.

When controversies exist in the Logos because of a lack of sufficient understanding, let us come together, separate what we agree on from what we disagree on, hold on to what we agree on, and with one accord, continue to research what we don't agree on. In this way, we keep the unity of the Spirit and avoid unnecessary conflicts that cause each to go his own way. In fact, there is only one Way. God promised us wisdom that clarifies our doubts. Let's consider the Scriptures below:

> 8 I desire therefore that the men pray everywhere, lifting up holy hands, without wrath and doubting; 9 in like manner also, that the women adorn themselves in modest apparel, with propriety and moderation, not with braided hair or gold or pearls or costly clothing, 10 but, which is proper for women professing godliness, with good works. 11 Let a woman learn in silence with all submission. 12 And I do not permit a woman to teach or to have authority over a man, but to be in silence. 13 For Adam was formed first, then Eve. 14 And Adam was not deceived, but the woman being deceived fell into transgression. 15 Nevertheless she will be saved in childbearing if they continue in faith, love, and holiness, with self-control (1 Timothy 2:8–15).

From verses 8 to 10, there's no problem. Almost all Bible-believing Christians agree on what those verses say. From verses 11 to 15, every group comes away with its own interpretation. Some stick to what Paul says. Others say the contrary—claiming Paul doesn't really mean what he says. In fact, some preachers jump into many historical and cultural explanations, which they claim reduce what Paul says to a Jewish tradition, even though the Bible doesn't talk about that. Keep in mind Paul speaks at the heart of the New Covenant. The biggest historical and cultural pattern or evidence we can have would be Jesus having a woman among the twelve or apostles laying hands on women to occupy spiritual leadership positions.

Am I against women? Certainly not. All I did was read the verses and look into a few historical facts. Truth is truth, different from what you get in modern feminist theories that have crept into the church. The truth is that women have their own roles they play in building the Body of Christ. Men can never compare to them in those roles. The contexts of the few exceptions such as Deborah, who judged Israel; Esther, who led the deliverance of the Jews; the elect lady John writes to in 2 John, and the four virgin daughters of Philip, the evangelist who prophesied, are not enough evidence to say Paul doesn't mean what he says.

Based on the current evidence, it appears that while God occasionally selected women to lead, He primarily chose men to be at the forefront. Deborah obviously understood this when she sent and called for Barak to deploy troops and lead the war against Sisera. Nonetheless, Barak, being scared to assume leadership in the war, requested Deborah's presence. Deborah clearly said, "I will surely go with you; nevertheless, there will be no glory for you in the journey you are taking, for the Lord will sell Sisera into the hand of a woman" (Judges 4:4-10). If leading wars was a natural role for women, there would be no need for her to mention it.

So, what is the solution? Stick to what the verses say and continue research until we find sufficient evidence that goes against what Paul says. We don't kill sorcerers today as commanded in the Old Testament because we have enough evidence from Jesus to help them know Him and be saved. We should look for reasonable biblical evidence that supports women in leadership positions in the church. In the absence of sufficient evidence, stick to what the Bible says. All those lengthy theological explanations instigate more confusion.

### Some Scriptures Need Additional Scriptures in the Same or Other Bible Books to Understand Them

Many Bible verses can survive on their own. Others are part of a topic. The topic may have verses scattered throughout the entire Bible. Although these verses may have a meaning of their own in the context in which the writer wrote them, you still need to consider them on the topic. Many sections of the Bible are stories or historical truths. One must read the entire passage to make meaning out of it. We are yet to make sufficient meaning out of a few verses and expressions in the Bible. For instance, Proverbs 18:1 says, "A man who isolates himself seeks his own desires; he rages against all wise judgment." This is a stand-alone verse. Of course, you can look for passages in the Bible that say something similar to it, but the verse is very explicit. You can write an entire book based on it.

Yet, when Solomon says, "Get wisdom! Get understanding!" in Proverbs 4:5, of course, the verse means what it says: encouraging us to get wisdom. However, it is better to read through the entire chapter because he explains why we should get wisdom. That is more helpful than sticking to the first statement, "Get wisdom!" The history of creation in Genesis, the lives of Moses, Joshua, and the children of Israel in the wilderness are historical truths. It is difficult to isolate verses from these passages, although there are some that point to specific areas of knowledge. The letters and gospels deal with various topics. Sometimes, a single verse deals with a topic. Other times, we must put together bits and pieces to understand what the writer communicates. To this day, we haven't really understood the expression, "it is easier for a camel to go through the eye of a needle than for a rich man to enter the kingdom of God" (Matthew 19:24).

## *Some Scriptures Speak to us Directly. Others are in the Bible for us to Learn From*

What did we say before? If you don't get the right meaning of a Scripture or section of the Bible (Logos), applying it becomes a gamble. One thing is of paramount importance at this stage: whether the Scripture or section relates to the Old or New Covenant. This is so important in interpreting Bible passages. This is where most unbiased theological research can help us. Why? Because inexperienced, immature, and proud Christians pick verses from all over the place and build theologies that don't match the relevant context. They expect others to agree with them.

Many Bible verses or sections of Scripture have a universal truth message, meaning they apply to all generations regardless of whether the writer wrote in the New or Old Testament. For instance, Genesis 1 tells us how God created everything. We can't say because we are children of the New Covenant, we will not believe the account of creation in the Old Testament Book of Genesis. In Exodus 20:8–11, God introduces the Sabbath law. The children of Israel walked with this law right up to the time of the Pharisees. However, in Matthew 12:1–14, Jesus shows this law wouldn't be useful to Christians in the New Covenant. In the Book of Hebrews and Letters of Paul to the Romans and Galatians, we learn it is impossible

147

to live by the Old Covenant Laws and please God. Those in the New Covenant have the liberty to serve God through grace in Jesus.

The same is true for the much-debated topic today: whether Christians should pay tithes or not. Tithing was a law in the Old Covenant. The New Testament introduces a greater and better ministry, liberal giving. That's why we don't see the apostles or early Christians paying tithes. Neither did they tell anyone to do so, nor did they receive such a command from Jesus. But we see believers going as far as selling their precious property (houses and lands) to help those of the faith who are in need among them.

Solomon lived in the Old Covenant, yet almost everything He wrote in the Books of Proverbs and Ecclesiastes applies to us today because they are universal principles of life that touch every generation. Yet even God's own direct Words in Exodus 22:18: "You shall not permit a sorceress to live," do not apply to those of us who are in the era of grace because Jesus tells us, "You have heard that it was said, 'You shall love your neighbor and hate your enemy. But I say to you, love your enemies, bless those who curse you, do good to those who hate you, and pray for those who spitefully use you and persecute you" (Matthew 5:43–44).

Let's analyze some parts of Psalm 91, which I believe many wrongly apply today. Forget about the disputes over who wrote it. It could have been Moses or David. Knowing the writer is useful, but the absence of this knowledge does not completely neutralize our understanding of the context. Verses one to four say;

> 1)He who dwells in the secret place of the Most High shall abide under the shadow of the Almighty. 2) I will say of the Lord, 'He is my refuge and my fortress; My God, in Him I will trust.' 3) Surely, He shall deliver you from the snare of the fowler and from the perilous pestilence. 4) He shall cover you with His feathers, and under His wings you shall take refuge; His truth shall be your shield and buckler.

These statements are universal. Regardless of which covenant you find yourself in, God is our refuge and fortress. But there is a difference in the way children of both covenants apply the statements. Let's get more context by analyzing further verses to bring out the difference. Verses five to eight say:

> 5) You shall not be afraid of the terror by night, nor of the arrow that flies by day, 6) Nor of the pestilence that walks in darkness, Nor of the destruction that lays waste at noonday. 7) A thousand may fall at your side, and ten thousand at your right hand; But it shall not come near you. 8) Only with your eyes shall you look and see the reward of the wicked."

149

The context tells us he who wrote Psalm 91 experienced danger in his life—a war situation. He finds himself in conditions he doesn't expect to come out victorious. When he talks about seeing "the reward of the wicked" in verse 8, he means enemies closed in, and they had no capacity to prevail against them. But with God on their side, what seems unbelievable becomes a reality.

What do we notice as we read through the Bible from the day God called Abraham to the time just before Nebuchadnezzar took the Jews captive in Babylon? They always fight wars against many nations, and God destroys wicked people. Let's look at a few examples. With just over three hundred people, Abraham fought against four kings who took his cousin Lot and family captives (Genesis 14:1–17). Abraham sees God destroy Sodom and Gomorrah (Genesis 19). Moses and the Israelites see God do wonders to deliver them from the hand of the Egyptians. Moses and Joshua fight many nations in the wilderness as they take the road to the Promised Land—Cannan. Joshua commands the sun and moon to stand still "over Gibeon" and "in the valley of Aijalon" to provide light for the Israelites on the battlefield. David strikes down lions and bears with his bare hands. On the battlefield, Adino the Eznite, the chief among David's captains, strikes down eight hundred adversaries at once. So, the writer of Psalm 91 drops these words with such a context at heart. The "eye for an eye" principle is the guide in his time. He rejoices seeing God fight for him and his people. God used him and his people to do wonders. He has seen God do unimaginable things to deliver them from trouble. Hence, he praises God.

It is sad to see Christians apply these verses as if they live in the same context as that of the writer. Some pray God destroys their enemies. Who are the enemies in the New Covenant you want God to destroy? Witches and wizards, homosexuals, serial murderers, rapists, the neighbor who puts poison in your food? Who? Where did Jesus lead a group to fight a physical war? How many physical battles did the apostles of Jesus and early Christian's fight? How does God want you to behave in front of those you consider your enemies? Call down fire from Heaven to consume them as Elijah did? Are many of us mistaken? You can clearly see Jesus' ministry of reconciliation is the total opposite of the "tooth for a tooth" thing. Jesus sends us out "as sheep in the midst of wolves." We should "be wise as serpents and harmless as doves" (Matthew 10:16). Yet, some Christians in this era of grace believe they would approach God's throne of grace in order for God to kill people. Although God can do that for His own pleasure, it is not our duty to request it. We've got a mission to use the Word of God and our attitude to bring people into His kingdom. "Let your light so shine before men, that they may see your good works and glorify your Father in Heaven" (Matthew 5:16).

In the old covenant, those who spread evil had to be eliminated to cleanse the land. Back then, that was how they performed deliverance. Some examples are the flood during Noah's time, the destruction of Sodom and Gomorrah, and the numerous wars fought by the Israelites to eradicate wicked nations. God frequently uses the phrase "cut off" to instruct Israel on dealing with sin among them.

Nowadays, Christians are equipped with the "word" and "ministry of reconciliation" and have received authority from Jesus to triumph over the enemy's power (Luke 10:19, 2 Corinthians 5:15-21). Through prayer and the Word of God, we fight a spiritual battle against evil, tearing down strongholds and overcoming anything that opposes Jesus (2 Corinthians 10:3-6). Jesus empowers us to rescue witches and wizards from witchcraft, free those trapped in occult practices, heal the most mysterious illnesses, and produce testimonies that astonish non-believers.

Can you see these differences? We can learn from verses 5 to 8 of Psalm 91, but we shouldn't apply them the same way as did he who wrote them. We are in a new and better covenant today—that of grace.

## *Scientific Research Can Improve our Knowledge of Some Scriptures or Sections of The Bible we Struggle With*

Let it be clear—the Bible can survive on its own with no additional external evidence. However, this does not mean that we should neglect historical, archaeological, or other scientific evidence that brings additional light to biblical claims. We are not stupid. We understand revelation and reason move together. The discovery of Bible parchments and the Dead Sea Scrolls helped to rectify some textual variants in earlier Bible translations that led to the modern ones. From studying history, we gain additional knowledge of the lifestyle of the Canaanites, ancient Babylon, the Roman Empire, and the Persian Kingdom to boost our understanding of what Scripture says. From the same history, we find plenty of evidence of non-believers who attest to the virgin birth, death, and resurrection of Jesus Christ. David asserts, "The heavens declare the glory of God; And the firmament shows His handiwork" (Psalm 19:1). Yet, astronomy, the study of celestial bodies, allows us to marvel at this beauty of God's creation in space.

## FOUR OTHER THINGS TO CONSIDER

Aside from everything we learned so far on Scripture interpretation, there are a few other basic things the reader should consider. We already saw common logic plays a vital role in helping us put Scriptures in their proper contexts. The things we'll mention in this section further strengthen this capacity. We want to be effective in using Bible passages. So, we want the foundation we build upon to be solid and authentic. Only then can we figure out how to properly apply Bible passages in our own contexts.

## WHAT JESUS DOES

Jesus is our model. He is the perfect example we want to emulate in our Christian walk. In all our endeavors, we want to match His will and actions. Paul says, "Imitate me, just as I also imitate Christ" (1 Corinthians 11:1). So, every time we come across a subject in the Bible, we want to know what Jesus did so we can imitate Him. Most of us are used to the question, "What would Jesus do?" When confronted with any topic, the first thing we do is analyze how Jesus approached it to determine how we would react in our own context. For instance, Jesus sets the perfect example of forgiveness by forgiving those who crucified Him. If He could forgive those who took away His life, He sets a standard that leaves us with no excuse for unforgiveness, come what may. Therefore, we can always look straight into His action to generate approaches for the issues we confront in our own lives.

## WHAT JESUS SAYS

It's important to keep in mind there was no Christian when Jesus was on earth. Many Christian theologians stumble on this point. Jesus was the only practitioner of a Christ-like life in those days. The Pharisees, Scribes, and Sadducees He confronted were not born again. Even His disciples did not understand His ministry the entire time they walked with Him. The people still depended on the laws of Moses, the Old Covenant. Jesus came to introduce the New Covenant. He used most of the entire three and a half years of His ministry to teach the people how to live as Christians. Yet, this new way to relate with God only became effective in people's lives in Acts 2, when the Holy Spirit descended upon His disciples.

Jesus says some things about some topics that relate directly to the New Covenant. The Sermon on the Mount in Matthew 5 is a good example. There, Jesus uses the phrase, "...you have heard that it was said." In such moments, He distinguishes between what the people believe at the moment and what is to come in the new life in Him. Hence, we know what we have to do in these verses because Jesus clearly says it. Other times, however, Jesus says things to bring people to reason, expose their wrong motives, and help them see the new faith life He introduces. This is the case when He confronts the Scribes and Pharisees. The laws of Moses shaped the mindsets of these people. Remember, they even stumbled many times on Moses' laws. But Jesus wants them to understand One greater than Moses or even Abraham is here, a Person who existed before the world. To expose their limitations

155

and introduce them to the new faith, Jesus confronts the foundations on which they built their current faith.

Hence, when Jesus discusses polygamy, adultery, marriage, and divorce with these religious leaders, the reader must understand He does nothing but try to help them see there's a new and better approach when faced with such problems. With these passages, we make a critical analysis to determine what applies to us today and what does not. Inexperience and overlearning cause some theologians to use such Scriptures to support divorce and polygamy, the ancient practices Jesus wants the people to abandon.

Sometimes, Jesus' actions speak to us directly. From them, we have a direct example of what to do in our own context. Other times, this direct act from Him does not exist, as with marriage. He was never married to a woman because the Church is His bride. He will marry us at the end of all things for eternity. When marriage troubles confront us, we can rely on what He says about marriage, but we must learn to carefully analyze and determine what applies to the Old and New Covenant.

# WHAT JESUS' APOSTLES

## AND EARLY BELIEVERS DO AND SAY

Everything Jesus does in the Bible serves as an example for us to follow. Remember, He lives a sinless life. We can never find a better example than Him. We know example is a better teacher than experience, although there are a few things about our ministry and life we will learn only from experience. Moreover, we notice there are situations for which there's no direct example from Jesus of how to behave, but He speaks about them, giving us either a direct command or a hint on what to do in our own context.

There are topics about which Jesus is silent in words and deeds or says very little. A good example is the physical church on earth. Remember, the Church starts with the apostles. While on earth, Jesus prepared minds for this new faith. In such cases, we look into the actions of the apostles and early Christians to determine what to do. The Bible says, "According to the grace of God, which was given to me, as a wise master builder, I have laid the foundation, and another builds on it. But let each one take heed of how he builds on it. For no other foundation can anyone lay than that which is laid, which is Jesus Christ" (1 Corinthians 3:10-11). Jesus comes and reveals the work of the kingdom. He outlays His plans for the kingdom project to His apostles. His apostles began the work by laying the foundation and starting to build on it. The early believers enjoyed direct leadership from the apostles— eyewitnesses of Jesus. That's why the Bible records the acts of these apostles and early believers so we can learn from them.

Whenever we can't find a direct answer from Jesus' acts or words, we can go to His apostles and early believers, see how they react, and learn from them. For instance, from them we learn about giving, as opposed to tithing, church administration, and many other things about the Christian lifestyle Jesus doesn't elaborate on.

## OTHER PARTS OF THE BIBLE

The last but not the least thing to consider is what other sections of the Bible say about the topic. Why is it important to consider this step last? Because there are two covenants in the Bible. If you neglect this fact, there's a high probability you'll interpret the passage out of context. Unbelievers pick verses here and there from both covenants, interpret them with bias, build their own theologies without the Holy Spirit's help, and try to attack the Christian faith. Inexperienced and over-learned theologians also collect and gather verses that seem best in their own eyes, build theologies that do not match our current settings, and expect everyone to agree with them. This is the reason for the divisions and segregations we have in the church community. As we said earlier, the Holy Spirit isn't the author of such confusion. He inspires diversity, not adversity and divisions. Intellectual pride brings us to contradicting viewpoints.

It is wise not to start with what other parts of the Bible say about the topic. Why? Because we "want to bring every thought to captivity to the obedience of Christ" (2 Corinthians 10:3-5). Saying this shouldn't call for polemics. We know the entire Bible is God's written Word and inspiration, but we are not foolish. We can distinguish between direct instructions God gives and things He inspires the writers to write for learning. There are instructions in the Old Covenant that still apply in the New. Many don't. We want to make that distinction. If you pick verses here and there, you become less effective in the process.

In those days, God's people killed witches, wizards, and those who practiced divination. That was right, according to the law. Nowadays, we preach the gospel to them and pray for their salvation. It was an eye for an eye, a tooth for a tooth. Today, we are bound to forgive and pray for those who persecute us. You don't go to the books of Deuteronomy, Leviticus, Isaiah, and the like; pick verses from there as you wish; and bring them to our current situation today. No, that's ridiculous. You must look into the context. Those people wrote to a particular audience in a specific context that may or may not apply to us today.

Therefore, you need a fair analysis to determine how to apply their words today. Remember, the Old Testament prepares the way for the New. Prophets in the Old Testament looked up to Jesus, even though they didn't understand His ministry. All they knew was something better was coming. Those of us who enjoy this better faith today look back at what Jesus did for us on the Cross of Calvary. Our faith for the future is strong because we look back at His finished work on the Cross of Calvary and the promises that follow.

The point of intersection for both the Old and New Covenants is Jesus' death and resurrection—the Cross of Calvary. In Him, we are all one; in the covenants, we are distinct. We must learn to bring out this difference when interpreting Bible passages to prevent unrealistic philosophies from enticing us. Hence, we start with Jesus' acts and then move to His words. If we can't find the anchor, we go to the apostles and early believers. Yet, if we still can't find the answer, we analyze other Bible passages about the issue, not ignoring the covenant in which the audience members whom the writer targets find themselves. If we do a fair analysis, the Holy Spirit guides us to find an answer that matches our context. There are very few of the Scriptures we will mishandle if we adopt this approach.

Sad to say, we have complicated Scripture interpretation with overlearning. The process shouldn't be that difficult. There's no reason for spiritual segregations over disputes on what the Logos means. Intellectual pride is the reason genuine children of God disagree over the few things they don't sufficiently understand in Scripture and go each his own way. Let's remember God doesn't encourage us to compromise our unity in the faith. He doesn't want us to agree to disagree. If we lack knowledge, let's ask Him. After all, what brings us together is far greater, a lot more, and better than the few things we dispute that separate us and reduce our efficacy in serving God.

# CONCLUSION

In the beginning, we said this little study is philosophical, the objective being to bring additional clarifications to two distinct things— the Bible and theology. The purpose of the study is to help us make better use of the Bible and the theologies it inspires. So we analyzed the Bible, its structure and content, and defined it as "a book that contains God's Word for humanity." We later said theology is "the method by which we seek and reason about God, His Word, and His will for humankind, organizing information and gathering evidence to understand Him better." We further outlined the different approaches theologians use to develop theologies and the types of theologies they develop. Then, we landed on the branches of good theology and explained how they add value to the Bible's content. Finally, we looked into the similarities and differences between the Bible and theology and saw ways to make better use of both. Then, we concluded with a practical approach to interpreting Scripture.

Let's nail everything down once and for all. The Bible and theology are two distinct things with a very close relationship. They are neither the same nor will they ever be rivals. It makes no sense to compare them. The Bible is the foundation of theology. It is greater than theology in all aspects because theology depends on it. Without the Bible's content, all theological explorations and thoughts are futile. Therefore, theology plays a complementary role to some of the Bible's content—when the Bible gives permission to do so and when there is a need for genuine research on our part.

Moreover, it is inefficient to preach theology. Rather, if we discover one, we teach it when necessary to bring more value to the Bible's content in a certain area. Furthermore, every theology must go through thorough scrutiny to figure out its added value in the light of Scripture before we accept it. It makes no sense for any theologian to boast about acquiring theological knowledge in an institution. Instead, every trained theologian has the responsibility of using the knowledge acquired to rightly divide the Word of Truth. It is inefficient, incorrect, improper, and less profitable for any theologian to promote a so-called school of thought. Aside from being the wrong thing for any theologian to do, such habits nourish unnecessary divisions and segregations in the church.

God called us to preach His Word in the Bible daily because in it is the power that leads to Jesus and salvation. Whenever we shift our focus from the primary role of preaching the Word of God to a non-organized engagement in theological arguments, we create confusion, disunity, and division in the Christian community. This wrong use of theology nourishes intellectual pride, which results in more harm to the Body of Christ than good.

May the Lord help us study His Word daily. May the Holy Spirit inspire the theologies that render the Great Commission more effective.

We pray in Jesus' Name, Amen!

> "Let no one deceive you with empty words, for because of these things the wrath of God comes upon the sons of disobedience. Therefore, do not be partakers with them" (Ephesians 5:6–7).

> "Beware lest anyone cheat you through philosophy and empty deceit, according to the tradition of men, according to the basic principles of the world, and not according to Christ" (Colossians 2:8).

> "In all things showing yourself to be a pattern of good works; in doctrine showing integrity, reverence, incorruptibility, sound speech that cannot be condemned, that one who is an opponent may be ashamed, having nothing evil to say of you" (Titus 2:7–8).

# CHRIST IN YOU

If you read this book and don't know Jesus, He wants to reveal Himself to you. He knocks on the door of your heart and wants to show you who He is. You can also become God's son or daughter and join God's household and family. All you have to do is surrender your selfish deeds and express your willingness to know more of Him. The Bible passages below explain how you do that:

> "… If you confess with your mouth the Lord Jesus and believe in your heart that God has raised Him from the dead, you will be saved. For with the heart one believes unto righteousness, and with the mouth confession is made unto salvation. For the Scripture says, "Whoever believes on Him will not be put to shame" (Romans 10:9–11).

> "Behold, I stand at the door and knock. If anyone hears My voice and opens the door, I will come into him and dine with him, and he with Me" (Revelations 3:20).

There are no rules. There is no equation. Just reflect on your past life and ask Him to come and guide you henceforth. It is all free. You don't pay money or give anything for salvation. The only thing you need after inviting Jesus is a Bible and fellowship around you in a Bible-believing church. God will perform the spiritual growth miracle in you. Soon, He'll use you to help others to come to the knowledge of the truth, too. Won't you take this opportunity God gives you today?

May the Good Lord guide your steps in Jesus' Name!

# REFERENCES

Abramson, Paul. *Defense of Creationism*, 1998.

Cherian, Saneesh. *General Introduction to the Bible*. Indus School of Apologetics and Theology Textbook. No.222R1.

Cheung, Vincent. *Systematic Theology*. 2010. http://www.vincentcheung.com

Clark, Harold W. *Creation Speaks, A Study of the Scientific Aspects of the Genesis Record of Creation and the Flood*. Pacific Press Publishing Association. 1947.

Crampton, W. Gary, and Bacon, Richard E. *Toward a Christian Worldview*. First Presbyterian Church of Rowlett, Texas, 2000.

Dembski, William A. *Science and Design*, First Things, #86, October 1, 1998.

Encyclopedia.com. *Testament in the Bible*. Encyclopedia.com. (n.d.). https://www.encyclopedia.com/religion/encyclopedias-almanacs-transcripts-and-maps/testament-bible#:~:text=In%20classical%20Latin%20the%20word,phrase%2C%20%22last%20will%20and%20testament

Harvestime International Institute. *Basic Bible Survey One, Old Testament*. Colorado Springs, 2007.

Keathley, J. Hampton III. *Bibliology, The Doctrine of the Written Word.* Biblical Studies Press, 1997.

Learning Bible. *How The Bible Came to Us.* Bible Society Making The Bible Heard.

Murrell, Stanford E. Th.D. *A Foundation for Faith. A n Introductory Study of Systematic Theology,* The Baptist Confession of Faith of 1689.

Mutia, Babila. *Performer, Audience, and Performance Context of Bakweri Pregnancy Rituals and Incantations.* 2005. https://journals.openedition.org/etudesafricaines/14932

Online Etymology Dictionary, apocrypha and Pseudepigrapha, https://www.etymonline.com/search?q=apocrypha, 2021-2024

Philip, Anand. *What is Philosophy.* Calvin Research Group, 2006.

Philip, Johnson C. *Resisting Mind Manipulation. Analyzing The Methods Which the World Uses to Fight Truth.* Calvin Research Group Academic Resource, Module 016A1.

Philip, Johnson C., and Cherian, Saneesh. *Analysis Of Mind Manipulation, Introduction To The Methods Which The World Uses To Fight Truth,* [Revised by Joe Giuffrida]. Calvin Research Group Academic Resource, Module 015A1.

Philip, Johnson C., and Cherian, Saneesh. *Analysis of Propaganda Techniques.* Research Group Academic Resource, Module 014A1.

Philip, Johnson C., and Cherian, Saneesh. *Analyzing Bible Difficulties*. Calvin Research Group Academic Resource, Module 012A1.

Philip, Johnson C., and Cherian, Saneesh. *Analyzing Errors of Interpretation*. Calvin Research Group Academic Resource, Module 011A1, Tools of Integrated Apologetics.

Philip, Johnson C., and Cherian, Saneesh. Calvin Research Group Academic Resource, *Module 003A1 Historical Apologetics, Historical/Legal Apologetics*.

Tchinda, N. V., Daihawe, D. L., Fotso, K. Sonfut, T. M., & Edjoh., *The Anthropological Study On The Bakweri*, 2012, https://anthgrp2.wordpress.com/

Tozer, A. W. He Is My All. *Living In The Faith Of God's Love For Me*, Second Edition, 2008.

Tozer, A. W., The Attributes of God Volume 1, *A Journey Into the Father's Heart*, February 2007.

# ABOUT JOHN MWAFISE WOLOKO

A humble servant of the Lord. Married to Amaya. Two wonderful girls, Elizabeth and Deborah and a brave boy, Joseph. Serves at the Regiogemeinde church of Riehen, Switzerland.

Earned a Bachelor of Ministry and Master of Divinity at the Trinity Graduate School of Apologetics and Theology, a Master of Advanced Studies in Humanitarian Logistics and Management at the University of Lugano, Switzerland.

Building Treff-End, a Christian NGO specializing in Christian social innovations.

Enjoys family, reading, writing, nature, sports, and excellent food.

NGO: www.treff-end.com

Blog: www.jmwoloko.treff-end.com

# ABOUT KHARIS PUBLISHING

Kharis Publishing, an imprint of Kharis Media LLC, is a leading Christian and inspirational book publisher based in Aurora, Chicago metropolitan area, Illinois. Kharis' dual mission is to give voice to under-represented writers (including women and first-time authors) and equip orphans in developing countries with literacy tools. That is why, for each book sold, the publisher channels some of the proceeds into providing books and computers for orphanages in developing countries so that these kids may learn to read, dream, and grow. For a limited time, Kharis Publishing is accepting unsolicited queries for nonfiction (Christian, self-help, memoirs, business, health and wellness) from qualified leaders, professionals, pastors, and ministers. Learn more at: https://kharispublishing.com/

www.ingramcontent.com/pod-product-compliance
Lightning Source LLC
Chambersburg PA
CBHW051424090426
42737CB00014B/2825